BURPEE AMERICAN GARDENING SERIES

GROUNDCOVERS

AMERICAN GARDENING SERIES

GROUNDCOVERS

Margaret Roach

PRENTICE HALL GARDENING

New York ◆ *London* ◆ *Toronto* ◆ *Sydney* ◆ *Tokyo* ◆ *Singapore*

PRENTICE HALL GENERAL REFERENCE
15 Columbus Circle
New York, NY 10023

Library of Congress Cataloging-in-Publication Data

Roach, Margaret.
      Groundcovers / Margaret Roach.
           p.   cm.—(Burpee American gardening series)
      Includes index.
      ISBN 0-671-84647-7
      1. Ground cover plants.   I. Title.   II. Series.
    SB432.R63   1993
      635.9′64—dc20   92-7621
                                              CIP

Designed by Patricia Fabricant and Levavi & Levavi
Manufactured in the United States of America

First Edition
10   9   8   7   6   5   4   3   2   1

Burpee is a registered trademark of
W. Atlee Burpee and Company.

PHOTOGRAPHY CREDITS

Agricultural Research Service, USDA: pp. 92–93
Cresson, Charles O.: pp. 47 top, 70 top
Pavia, Jerry: pp. 46 top, 49 bottom
W. Atlee Burpee & Co.: pp. 32, 76 top, 79 top, 88

Line drawings by Michael Gale: pp. 36, 37, 40, 86, 87
and by Elayne Sears: p. 39
Horticultural editor: Suzanne Frutig Bales

Cover: *At New York Botanical Garden in New York City, designer Lynden Miller contrasts foliar textures and colors of lamb's ears, coreopsis 'Moonbeam', blue oat grass, sedum 'Autumn Joy' and Russian sage.*

Preceding pages: *Even the most common of groundcovers needn't be dull. In the Pennsylvania garden of Charles Cresson, a bed of the showy variety of* Pachysandra terminalis *called Variegata' brightens the shade cast by trees.*

CONTENTS

INTRODUCTION

Plant as I might—and anyone who knows me will verify that I have dug a lot of holes the last few years—I found my yard was becoming more of a plant collection than a coherent landscape. What was essentially a living record of years of nursery visits and shopping sprees at botanical garden plant sales stood before me, but as I was regularly reminded by wiser gardeners, an assortment of plants does not a garden make.

In short, what I needed was to connect the dots: to find some way to tie together the dwarf rhododendrons and the century-old lilacs in whose shade I had planted them; the newly placed viburnum and variegated red-twig dogwood with the grand, vintage cedar that stood nearby; and even the jumble of perennials in my ever-expanding flower beds.

Unless I acted with unfailing diligence, what tied them together more often than not was weeds—not exactly the groundcover of choice and anything but consistent looking. Dock and thistle, witchgrass and bindweed, all of them fully intending to take over if permitted.

These days, I jump right in *before* the weed seeds and creeping rootstocks have a chance, seizing the chance myself by introducing one groundcover or a mix of these important plants to each bare patch of earth. Not only am I weeding a lot less, but the place is starting to look as if someone actually planned it.

The foreground of the flower gardens, where border meets lawn, is now happily carpeted in a mosaic of purple (bugleweed), silver (lamb's ears) and chartreuse (lady's-mantle). The cracks between pavers of the front walk teem with thymes and woolly yarrow instead of spotted spurge and purslane. I am no longer fighting to muscle the mower 'round every last tree and shrub in the place individually, because most of them are now integrated into big islands, with sweeps of such favorite low-maintenance groundcovers as ferns, hostas and astilbe at their feet.

Groundcovers can also be liberating in a more significant way. Never before have they been so appealing from an ecologic and economic standpoint. With time, money and natural resources at a premium, these are the plants of preference for busy gardeners wishing to adhere to the principles of a planetary conscience.

I feel strongly that each of us is steward of his or her own little corner of the landscape, a privilege that comes with the return obligation to treat the place in which we live with love and respect. To use chemicals in gardening is completely out of sync with this essential force, an act of hubris, I believe, and about as sensible as pouring gasoline on your granola. Which brings us to the subject of the great American lawn.

Like many Americans of the postwar generations, I grew up in suburbia, a child reared on the indelible character (and with the stained knees) of a community of green grass lawns. Today, however, I look at the lawn as a liability, a chemical-, fuel- and water-guzzling dinosaur that needs to be rethought.

If the ground at your place is carpeted in wall-to-wall lawn, perhaps it is time to make room for at least some area rugs of alternative groundcover. Before long, I expect you'll be lifting more turf, as I am, and planting more of the low-growing shrubs, perennials, herbs and vines that are better choices.

Even if I had an excess of time and no concern about environmentally wasteful or hazardous practices, I'd turn to groundcovers on the basis of aesthetic considerations alone. I'd much rather spend my weekends looking out at an expanse of astilbe or ginger, lamb's ears or bearberry, perennial geranium or, yes, even plain old, boring pachysandra than I would hefting the noisy, nasty old mower over all that lawn.

So what groundcover will it be? A meadow full of wildflowers, a thyme lawn that bursts forth fragrance with every footstep, a low, damp area brightened with variegated Japanese sweet flag or marsh marigolds? Start to think in terms of the possibilities of groundcovers, and the only limit is the reaches of your imagination.

A springtime effusion including phlox, ferns, primroses and columbine brightens the Redfield garden in Connecticut.

IN ON THE GROUND FLOOR

Although groundcovers are the lowest tier of the complex outdoor picture, don't be tricked into regarding them as lowly. The bunchberry (*Cornus canadensis*) of the New England woodland floor, the little bluestem (*Schizachyrium scoparium*) and coneflower (*Ratibida columnifera*) of the Midwestern prairie, the dune grasses of our coastlines, these are groundcovers all, and hardly insignificant.

Quite to the contrary, they are more often the foundations of the entire landscape. If they are foundations in nature, then in the garden, groundcovers are the floor covering on which the rest of the living furniture rests, a unifying factor with the potential to tie together the whole decor. Even the tiniest garden, one grown in a pot or window box, is vastly improved with the addition of a groundcover such as lobelia or sweet alyssum, for they give the miniature design a cohesiveness it could not otherwise possess.

Whatever the site, containers included, groundcovers serve various ecologically important functions, too: As living mulch, they safeguard the soil from erosion, extremes of heat and cold, and from moisture loss. They provide shelter and nesting sites for various birds and small mammals, plus fruit or seeds for those same creatures and pollen and nectar for bees and butterflies.

Take a walk in any botanical garden and you will see right away what horticultural professionals have long known: Groundcovers are essential unifiers and time-savers. Unfortunately, decades of relentless, uninspired massing of the most common of groundcovers other than turf grass—the "big three" of ivy, pachysandra and periwinkle (*Vinca minor*)—in office park after office park and front yard after front yard have inadvertently slandered this whole category of diverse and versatile plants.

Say *groundcover*, and most people think of a plague of pure green pachysandra, pachysandra and more pachysandra, blanketing practically everything in its path from sidewalk to foundation. Much the way our postwar penchant for rigid foundation planting has made such worthy shrubs as yew and photinia into clichés, the monotonous, formulaic use of the plainest forms of a few easily propagated creepers has led to their dishonor, too. But the blame here should be assigned to the humans who did the planting, not to the plants themselves.

It's time to elevate these ground-level subjects to higher status, which will at last improve our home landscapes to more than cookie-cutter imprints of one another. What this requires is that gardeners take the time to learn to use a wider palette of groundcover plants and the best-looking forms of each one that can be found. But first, let's backtrack and get down some of the basics of working with groundcovers.

Groundcovers should be beautiful even when there are no flowers. At New York Botanical Garden (clockwise from grass at rear), blue Lyme grass, perennial geranium, silvery lamb's ears, variegated lilyturf and the red of Japanese barberry mingle in a handsome tapestry of color, form and texture.

FORMS AND FUNCTIONS

*A glade of hay-scented fern (*Dennstaedtia punctilobula*) unfurls to form a fresh green carpet in time for the azaleas.*

*Bunchberry (*Cornus canadensis*) is an American native groundcover, an integral element in northeastern forests. Its flowers resemble those of dogwood, to which it is related.*

What exactly is a groundcover? Most any plant will cover the ground if you plant enough of it close together to start, or wait around long enough for it to fill the gaps at its own pace. Depending on your perspective, a mature grove of 10-foot-tall rhododendron could be considered a groundcover planting, as could the quick-sprawling vines of a summertime pumpkin patch, or even a whole farm field of winter wheat or rye destined to be turned under as soil-building "green manure" come the first signs of spring.

The distinctions sometimes blur in other ways, too. When we mass astilbes under a tree, we call this a groundcover; in the flower bed, we simply call a grouping of the same plant perennials. And are those Bar Harbor junipers holding the bank at the beach house shrubs or groundcovers?

The confusion stems from the fact that the term *groundcover* is not so much a botanical one as a horticultural one. It tells us what the plant can do—what its application in the garden is from a practical standpoint. When we speak of groundcovers in the purest sense, what we are referring to is any plant inclined by its habit and rate of growth to get the job of covering the ground done enthusiastically, whatever botanical category of plant it may fit into.

Groundcovers hail from wide-ranging corners of the plant world. Some, cotoneaster and the dwarf rhododendrons, for example, are really woody shrubs; others are subshrubs more often associated with the herb garden, such as rosemary and thyme. The astilbe mentioned above and daylilies, to name two of many examples, are typically classed among the flower border's herbaceous perennials (herbaceous meaning that their tissue is soft, not woody, and typically dies to the ground or thereabouts each winter).

There are vining plants well suited to covering the ground, too. These are usually such woody plants as ivy (*Hedera* species) and roses (*Rosa wichuraiana*, to name one low grower). And there are even bulbs that would make a grand groundcover display—among them daffodils, wood hyacinths and *Anemone blanda*—provided their typical single season of interest isn't a liability from a design standpoint.

So far the plants mentioned, woody and herbaceous alike, perform in a perennial fashion, living from season to season over many years, while increasing in size or population. But annuals—those plants that grow from seed all the way through the life cycle to produce a fresh crop of seed themselves in a single season—can also be used as groundcovers. Sowing a packet of sweet alyssum seeds below your roses, for instance, will provide a fast, long-blooming carpet to complete the rose-garden picture in style.

HOW DOES YOUR GROUNDCOVER GROW?

What a gardener will want to know most is what a plant's leaves and flowers look like, and indeed, catalog descriptions and illustrations of them can be positively intoxicating—particularly after a long winter with little or no green in sight. But a plant's architecture is at least as important, particularly in the case of groundcovers, whose more horizontal than vertical habit makes them such good candidates for the job at hand.

More than any other physical factor, height is the one to consider when planning the bottom tier of the landscape, because the scale of the lowest layer must either correspond to the existing elements or serve to anchor elements to follow.

Whether a particular plant is a shrub, subshrub or vine is not so much to the point as answering the question of how tall a potential groundcover will grow. For the purpose of this book, only plants 2 feet high or shorter will be examined in detail (an exception: some of the ornamental grasses discussed on page 61), as many larger ones fit more specifically into the category of perennials, annuals or flowering shrubs—other titles already available to interested gardeners as part of the *Burpee American Gardening Series*.

On the subject of height, a caveat: Cuttings from the very same plant subsequently grown under differing conditions can result in two very different-size

Intermediate Shrubs for Groundcover

Although not detailed in the Plant Portraits, these shrubs are good groundcover candidates for a somewhat taller effect.

Berberis species (barberry)
Cephalotaxus species (plum yew)
Deutzia gracilis (deutzia)
Euonymous alata (burning bush)
Forsythia × *intermedia* 'Arnold Dwarf' (forsythia)
Genista species (broom)
Leucothoe species (leucothoe)
Mahonia aquifolium (mahonia)
Nandina domestica (heavenly bamboo)
Pieris japonica (pieris)
Rhododendron species
Rosa rugosa, R. virginiana, R. Wichuraiana (roses)
Skimmia japonica (skimmia)
Spiraea species (spirea)
Stephanandra incisa (stephanandra)
Taxus baccata, T. cuspidata (yew)

A happy jumble of Vinca, strawberry, Lamiastrum *and sweet woodruff is suitably romantic to accompany a shady corner.*

What is a groundcover? From low-lying mosses and lawn grasses to plants with the stature and colorful flowers of rhododendron, the possibilities are almost limitless.

*Many flowering herbaceous perennials such as daylilies (*Hemerocallis*) make fine groundcover choices.*

plants; hence the range of height typically indicated in reference books and here, too. The quality of the soil and the amount of light, water and nutrients a plant receives can dramatically affect its performance. And a plant grown in the same garden year after year may vary, too; an unusually hot or dry season can retard growth, and repeated late frosts can nip plants in the bud one too many times for total recovery and peak output that year. (Even flower color can be affected by vagaries of weather and culture or placement, particularly soil moisture.

For instance, the popular sedum cultivar *Sedum spectabile* 'Autumn Joy' will have darker red flowers in dry soil and paler in moist. Many flowers will be washed out by direct sun, being at their best in indirect light or shade.)

Knowing how tall a plant will grow isn't enough to make a choice, of course. In addition to its eventual height range, just how does your groundcover grow on the horizontal plane? Giving a plant's habit of growth careful consideration is essential, and here again, groundcovers are a diverse lot indeed.

Hostas, astilbes and ferns are well suited to covering the ground in less-than-sunny spots.

Ornamental grasses like Miscanthus sinensis *'Striatus' require relatively little maintenance.*

There are carpeters, creepers and sprawlers among them, and these tend to be the lowest groundcovers of all. Some, like *Ajuga reptans* or *Phlox subulata*, form dense mats. Others, such as *Lamiastrum galeobdolon*, prefer to cascade in a looser, trailing fashion. There are clump-forming groundcovers (*Heuchera*); ones that make near-perfect mounds (some of the bigger hostas and *Artemisia schmidtiana* 'Silver Mound', so aptly named); and others whose inclination it is to weave airily through anything and everything with which they come into contact (clematis).

Yes, clematis is a wonderful groundcover, or to be more precise, it is wonderful when used in tandem with another groundcover; threaded through a prostrate evergreen, for example, it is just the right icing on the cake. An artist with a vast garden near the seashore lets clematis spill over plants right into his pathways, too, softening edges and setting a mood you might call romantic chaos. Most vines make good groundcovers if encouraged to sprawl rather than climb.

Another key consideration when selecting a groundcover is whether it is evergreen (holds its leaves throughout the year) or deciduous. Although the quality of dropping its leaves or going completely dormant for a third or even half the year or more may be tolerable in certain spots in the garden, in prominent locations there is often no substitute for the evergreen nature of other groundcovers. Hence the unparalleled popularity of that easy-to-grow, over-used threesome, ivy, pachysandra and vinca. If only more gardeners knew the virtues of the numerous evergreen gingers, hellebores and ferns equally as well!

Some attention should also be given to the amount of care that will be required by one plant as opposed to another. Certain plants' easy-care attributes score lots more points than other fussier, labor-intensive ones. A low-growing, flowering perennial or annual that requires diligent deadheading of spent flowers might make a good groundcover part of the time, but without hours of regular maintenance it may look awful. Choose another plant instead. After all, isn't the prospect of liberation from a portion of the drudgery of garden maintenance a reason for turning to groundcovers in the first place?

This California hillside is carpeted with drought-tolerant, evergreen Baccharis pilularis, *set off by a ground-level planting of colorful massed perennials.*

In the garden of landscape designer Neil Jorgensen of Harvard, Massachusetts, mixed broadleaf evergreens flank gravel pathways.

GROUNDCOVERS AT WORK

Groundcovers are the real work-horses of the plant world. Besides their ability to tie together the layers of the landscape beautifully, groundcovers are problem solvers in many other ways. Among their many potential talents:

◆ To unify a design by filling in the foreground of a flower garden, for example, or linking otherwise disparate elements such as trees and shrubs into coherent islands of pattern, color and texture.

◆ To soften hard edges of the landscape, as a low border along paths or driveways can, for example, or beside a building. Except in the most formal, austere planting scheme, too many hard lines look anything but natural; groundcovers can blur some of those sharp edges beautifully.

◆ To act as a living mulch, protecting the soil beneath them from compaction by rain, baking by sun and other physical stresses.

◆ To insulate the ground and act as a thermal blanket for companion plants, such as bulbs, shrubs and perennial flowers, helping to reduce heaving.

◆ To reduce water requirements of companion plants by shading their "feet" and slowing evaporation of available moisture from the soil.

◆ To help generate humus. Groundcovers trap debris such as fallen leaves and twigs beneath them and allow slow decomposition of this material. Think of the plants of the forest floor; this is the original recipe for compost, without bins but using groundcover plants as the holding devices.

◆ To reduce watering, mowing, fertilizer and other chemical usage compared with traditional turf grass.

◆ To check erosion, particularly on cliffs, dunes and other steep places, as well as in exposed, windswept areas. The rooting habits of certain groundcovers—those such as *Pachysandra* that are suckering (that spread by underground stolons or shoots) or ones that root along their stems wherever they touch moist soil, such as creeping cotoneaster (*Cotoneaster adpressus*) and paxistima (*Paxistima canbyi*) —make them especially good for this purpose. The much-hated native American groundcover poison ivy (*Toxicodendron radicans*) possesses an ambitious root system that has long served to stabilize soil of such coastal areas as Long Island, preventing them from washing away.

◆ To hide ripening foliage from bulbs and other short-season plants. Slow-to-awaken *Ceratostigma plumbaginoides*, for instance, is hardly out when

Hostas, in flower or not, are among the finest of herbaceous perennials for groundcover.

grape hyacinth and other early spring bulbs do their thing, but thickens up in summer and then puts on its own show mixing showy red stems and indigo flowers. Even more common groundcovers like pachysandra can perform this task ably, and the use of bulbs with them certainly uplifts an otherwise mundane mass at least part of the year. Better yet, underplant them in a bed of variegated pachysandra.

◆ To hide unsightly "legs" or "feet" of certain plants. Consider a blanket of big-root geranium (*Geranium macrorrhizum*) under such twiggy shrubs as forsythia and mock orange, or a silvery wave of *Artemisia* ×'Powis Castle' camouflaging the ground-level portion of *Crambe cordifolia*.

◆ To reduce time and materials used in garden maintenance, as groundcovers don't require mowing the way lawn does.

◆ To reduce time spent in weeding. Groundcovers shade the soil, depriving many weed seeds of the light required for germination. Once the groundcover fills in, it also simply chokes out many unwanted invaders.

◆ To draw the eye to a specimen tree or shrub by planting a living doily beneath it, such as *Cyclamen coum* in the dry shade of a pine or *Pulmonaria saccharata* under a variegated weigela.

◆ To carpet an area where you can't mow, because of exposed tree roots, for instance, or rocky protrusions, or because it is too steep.

◆ To carpet where grass won't grow, under the dense shade of a tree, for example, or in extremely shady or dry locations. Many beautiful groundcovers are perfectly content to grow in partial, if not deep, shade; relatively few lawn grasses will endure shady exposures.

◆ To hold a place temporarily while other plants (young woody plants or herbaceous perennials) fill in, blocking out weeds in the meantime. Annuals such as begonia and impatiens, or tender bulbs grown as annuals in many areas, such as oxalis or caladium, should be used for this purpose, because they are fast covering. The former, because they are seed grown, are most economical.

The nooks and crannies formed between terra-cotta pavers are perfect homes for such tiny groundcovers as creeping mint (Mentha requienii).

SPACE INVADERS: BULLIES OR A BLESSING?

Can a groundcover do its job too well? Some are positively unstoppable—a blessing in the right spot, an eternal nightmare in the garden proper, or up against the lawn in the case of some insidious turf infiltrators. It is said that no plant is a

Baby's tears (Soleirolia soleirolii), shown with Maranta, is a good candidate for tight spots.

match for a gardener armed with a spade, but in the case of certain vigorous botanical creatures, it seems the plants didn't hear the part about their being outmatched.

A warning: Size is no indication of strength. Even tiny, charming-looking plants such as creeping veronica (*Veronica filiformis*) can be positive monsters. Cute as it is, *V. filiformis* has escaped cultivation and is now a major lawn pest in the northeast United States and Canada.

Then there are regional factors, including climate and soil, to be considered. A plant that behaves like a delicate specimen in the sandy soil of Long Island may be a positive weed in the moist, agreeable Pacific Northwest. Heavy clay soils and the extreme heat of the Southeast can prove too much for a plant that would be happy to romp over an entire moist woodland floor in New England, if given the chance.

Realities of climate make a big difference in how easy or hard it is to control an aggressive plant. At the northernmost edge of its hardiness range, where it may die back to the ground each winter, it may be possible to contain even the notorious bamboos, which in gentler zones will even cross a driveway or shallow cement foundation with their eager underground rhizomes.

Hay-scented fern (*Dennstaedtia punctilobula*), for instance, and certain of the wormwoods (*Artemisia ludoviciana* 'Silver King' and 'Silver Queen', to name two) are very useful groundcovers in certain situations, low-care perennials with a robust, spreading nature. In light soils or a small garden, though, each can prove itself quickly unwelcome. Handle with care in such a situation, or better yet, select another fern or another *Artemisia* instead. Even the wonderful family of mints (*Mentha* species) and the related bee balm or bergamot (*Monarda* species) can be a nuisance in the confines of a formal garden design, although they are far easier to pull out when the time comes than either the fern or the wormwood.

Some species of groundcovers and vining plants should simply never be planted. Already they are proving to be noxious weeds in various regions of the country, and should not be encouraged. One need only have seen kudzu in the South to imagine the disastrous effect. Bittersweet (*Celastrus scandens*), for example, wild grape, the Hall's honeysuckle (*Lonicera japonica* 'Halliana'), Japanese knotweed (*Polygonum cuspidatum*), the all-green form of porcelain berry (*Ampelopsis brevipedunculata*) and the green goutweed (*Aegopodium podagraria*) are among the thugs.

Others such as *Petasites japonicus* (an extremely large-leaved Japanese foliage plant with edible, asparaguslike flowers early in the growing season) can be valuable for rapid and dramatic covering of large areas. It is happy in shade, and tolerates damp spots, too. Few groundcovers are so stately, and in any garden with an Asian inspiration, it's a must. But *Fuki*, as it is called in Japan, has unmatched zeal and so a site must be evaluated carefully with an eye to this plant's amazing future potential. Either that or plan to dig out any and all young offsets where they are not wanted—right away, before they get a better foothold and the better of you.

A PLANT FOR EVERY PLACE

One of the gardening maxims I find myself repeating is "Don't fight the site." The temptation to plant in the face of reason is sometimes great, but one needs to resist, or be content to grow a plant as an annual and write off the casualty without remorse at season's end. But right-plant-right-place wisdom is the basis of horticultural success, and best heeded. Before I let myself get hooked on how great a nursery container of lamb's ears (*Stachys byzantina*) looks next to another of the purple-and-silver-splotched Japanese painted fern (*Athyrium goeringinanum* 'Pictum'), I need to ask myself one bottom-line question: How will each one fare if I try to grow them in the same spot? (Not well, because the *Stachys* is a real worshiper of the kind of full sunlight that by midsummer will burn the fern to a crisp.)

Most of all, this means how much light, and what kind of light, will be available to candidates for the spot I am considering. If you are shopping for plants in early spring (or mail-ordering them in winter for spring delivery) you will have to rely on memory to determine the light conditions of the area in which you intend to put the plants. Because the sun's position in the sky is so different during the low-light seasons and, as trees have lost their leaves in many areas during winter, too, it is impossible to go out and evaluate light for summer. I gather hints from what else is growing there, shade plants or sun lovers, tall shrubs and trees that may cast shadows, and so forth. Another clue: If there is lawn growing on the spot, and it is thick, healthy and green in the active season, there is probably at least a half-day of sun.

The most helpful garden centers, to my mind, arrange their plants in two groups, according to light requirements, and then alphabetically within those categories of sun and shade. Plants that can go either way should be offered in both places. This way, shopping becomes an educational experience for the gardener, and the purchases have a better chance of survival. Grouping plants simply as "sun" and "shade" is an overgeneralization, of course. Many "shade" plants will grow

in sun, sometimes even full sun, if the soil is continually moist. Lady's-mantle (*Alchemilla mollis* or *A. vulgaris*), for instance, is normally rated for part shade, but is happy in many areas in a moist, sunny spot. The sensitive fern (*Onoclea sensibilis*) is another such example. The equation of a plant's ideal position has more to it than light alone; available moisture and soil quality (organic content, pH and drainage) are the next most important factors.

Groundcovers for Hot, Arid Climates

Arctostaphylos species (manzanita, bearberry)
Arctotheca calendula (capeweed)
Asparagus densiflorus 'Sprengeri' (asparagus fern)
Baccharis pilularis (coyote brush)
Dichondra micrantha (dichondra)
Gazania ringens (gazania)
Genista species (broom)
Juniperus species (juniper)
Mesembryanthemum species (ice plant)
Opuntia species (prickly pear)
Phyla nodifloria canescens (creeping lippia)
Potentilla verna (spring cinquefoil)
Rosmarinus officinalis 'Prostratus' (rosemary)
Santolina chamaecyparissus (gray lavender cotton)
Teucrium chamaedrys (germander)
Verbena rigida (verbena)
Vinca major (greater periwinkle)

Cracks in the Pavement: Groundcovers for Tight Spots

A stone path or patio can be just that—or it can be the opportunity to create a garden in miniature. Many of the matlike growers are tiny enough to tuck into the cracks, where they will help stabilize the stones while crowding out weeds.

Acaena microphylla (New Zealand bur)
Achillea tomentosa (woolly yarrow)
Antennaria species (pussytoes)
Anthemis nobilis (chamomile)
Arenaria species (sandworts)
Aubretia deltoidea (rock cress)
Cerastium tomentosum (snow-in-summer)
Dianthus deltoides (maiden pink)
Dichondra micrantha (dichondra)

Draba aizoides (whitlow grass)
Hedyotis caerulea or *Houstonia caerulea* (bluets)
Mazus reptans (mazus)
Mentha requienii (creeping mint)
Moss (various genera and species)
Papaver alpinum (alpine poppy)
Phlox species (creeping phlox)
Sagina subulata (Irish moss)
Sedum acre and *S. spurium* 'Dragon's Blood' (sedum or stonecrop)
Soleirolia soleirolii (baby's tears)
Thymus species (thyme)
Tripleurospermum tchihatchewii (turfing daisy)
Verbena × *hybridum* and others (verbena)
Veronica saturjoides and *V. prostrata* (speedwell)

HERBS

Some of the most rewarding groundcover choices are those we usually call herbs. Depending on species, they may offer us such qualities as aromatic foliage, a supply of useful flowers and cuttings (for cooking and teas or for fresh and dried arrangements and potpourri). They are generally durable plants, uncomplaining even in relatively lean soils; most require a sunny exposure and a well-drained spot for peak performance (the exceptions that prefer a bit of shade and somewhat moister soil are starred in the box to the right).

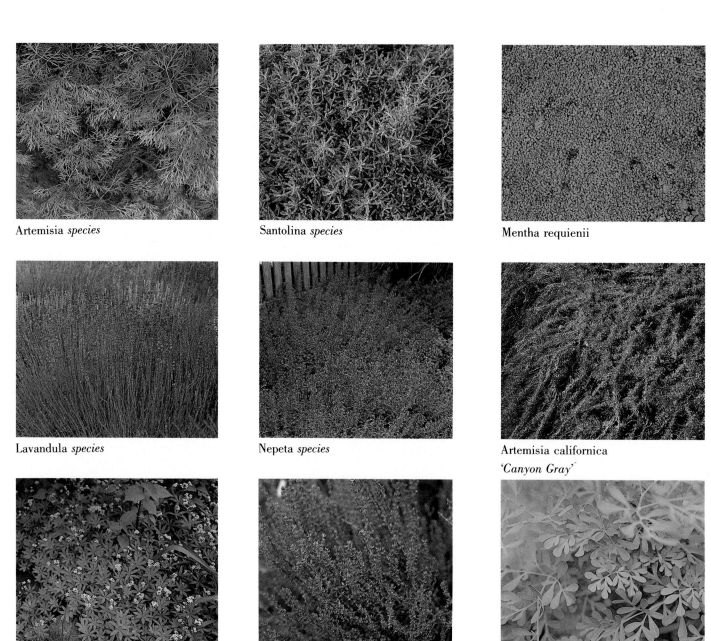

Artemisia *species*

Santolina *species*

Mentha requienii

Lavandula *species*

Nepeta *species*

Artemisia californica
'Canyon Gray'

Galium odoratum

Thymus *species*

Ruta *species*

Groundcovers from the Herb Garden

Achillea tomentosa (woolly yarrow)

Alchemilla mollis* (lady's-mantle)

Artemisia species (artemisia)

Ballota pseudodictamnus (ballota)

Chamaemelum nobile (*Anthemis nobilis*, chamomile)

Galium odoratum* (sweet woodruff)

Herniaria glabra (rupturewort)

Lavandula species (lavender)

Mentha species* (mint)

Nepeta mussinii (catmint)

Origanum vulgare 'Aureum' (creeping golden oregano)

Rosmarinus species (rosemary)

Ruta species (rue)

Salvia species (garden sage)

Santolina species (lavender cotton)

Satureja montana (winter savory)

Stachys byzantina (lamb's ears)

Teucrium chamaedrys (germander)

Thymus species (thyme)

DESIGNING WITH GROUNDCOVERS

MIX, DON'T MATCH

The garden I grew up with was a suburban American classic: lawn and pachysandra on the ground level, yews (clipped, of course), rhododendron and dogwood above. In spring, an island bed of red tulips followed purple crocuses. Each summer, marigolds and zinnias took their place in gay—some might say garish—style. But more than anything else, the place was just plain green.

When I set out years later to make my own, first garden, I had a very hard time breaking away from such a rigid image as the one of my childhood front yard (and the yard of virtually every home in my block, neighborhood and perhaps region). Today, though, my garden is more crazy quilt than solid-colored bedspread, a fact that makes me happy—at least most of the time. But the process of loosening up and just allowing myself to try things in the spirit of come what may, without recrimination, hasn't been easy.

Beginning gardeners, held back by a lack of confidence and the limited selections of outlets where they first shop for plants, may resort to the safety of the same old reliables. But a bag of grass seed, a boxed hybrid tea rose, a flat of ivy and a six-pack of impatiens doesn't go very far in creating a dream landscape, and before long, such basics don't satisfy the gardener's fast-growing passion, either. Start taking some risks, or risk boring yourself right out of an interest in gardening. First, have a good look around the place. An ability to design success-fully with plants starts with honing the capacity to see not just the big stuff, but every last one of the tiniest details. Take notes of what you like, what you don't, what colors look bad or good to you when paired. You should not only do this in your own garden (or garden-to-be) but also make time for stops at other houses that catch your eye (whether for their beauty or beastliness), at public gardens and even along highway medians, where some truly low-care groundcover plantings are being installed to meet realities of lower state budgets and work-force reductions.

For most of us, the prospect of mixing patterns, colors and textures calls up panicky recollections of pulling together an outfit at the last moment for an important occasion or selecting paint and wallpaper single-handedly for a new home. Although few would say a plaid shirt, a striped pair of pants and a jacket that matched neither "worked" or that a fuchsia-and-red color scheme conjured images of their dream kitchen, gardening allows for much wider interpretation. Loosen up and enjoy it. After all, nature wears pink with purple for spring, orange with red for fall and mismatched greens all year 'round, and everybody gapes at the splendor.

It's especially important to break away from the safest, most predictable options with groundcovers, because more often than not, you'll be planting large areas. As we've discussed, big areas of a single plant are usually boring, and sometimes disastrous, too. If you plant only

In the back garden of Long Island landscape designer Connie Cross and nurseryman Jim Cross, the lawn was reduced by the creation of mounded beds featuring heaths and heathers.

Euonymous and suffer a serious infestation of euonymous scale, what will you have to show for your efforts when every last infested branch must be cut back, or every plant removed? A mixed planting scheme can lessen the impact that disease can have on your garden's appearance.

Spacing of 20 Common Groundcovers

Here are some suggested spacings for popular ground-covers, assuming you can wait about three years for plants to knit together; plant tighter for faster coverage.

Ajuga: 12 to 18 inches

Artemisia: 18 to 24 inches

Asarum: 8 to 12 inches

Astilbe: 12 to 24 inches

Bergenia: 18 to 24 inches

Brunnera: 18 to 24 inches

Convallaria: 6 to 12 inches

Epimedium: 12 to 18 inches

Gazania: 12 inches

Hedera: 12 to 18 inches

Helleborus: 12 to 18 inches

Hemerocallis: 18 to 24 inches

Heuchera: 18 inches

Hosta: 12 to 24 inches

Lamium: 18 to 24 inches

Liriope: 8 to 18 inches

Lysimachia: 12 to 18 inches

Pachysandra: 12 to 18 inches

Sedum: 12 inches

Stachys: 12 to 18 inches

---

*Variegated leaves like those of goutweed (*Aegopodium podagraria *'Variegata') bring the illusion of light to shady spots.*

SHADES OF GREEN

What color is the landscape? Much of the time the right answer is "basically green," but that's an incomplete answer. Have you ever taken a close look at what nature offers up in the way of green and how much the same plant changes in hue throughout the growing season.

All too often, people want to talk about flowers: when, what color, how long lasting. I won't do that here, at least not right now. When beginning to think out a design, focus on the foliage first and foremost, as it will be in place from about half the year to year 'round, depending on factors of species and climate.

The fact that leaves generally outlast flowers by a wide margin is no accident. Plants exist on photosynthesis, a process undertaken in the chloroplasts, tiny bodies within plant cells where the green pigment chlorophyll is located. In photosynthesis, plants use light energy to produce food from carbon dioxide and water.

Flowers, on the other hand, are reproductive organs, a bonus for enhancing the garden picture, but in most cases a relatively short phase a plant goes through in each growing cycle (if left unchecked by human intervention like mowing, and given sufficient light, moisture and nutrients to yield blooms). Flowers may be miraculously beautiful to look at, but foliage is the gardener's best friend. Learn to appreciate the subtleties of leaf form, color and texture and you will find that you advance quickly in your ability to design.

Because green is the blending of yellow and blue, there are greens in which one component or the other has the upper hand. The blue-greens are cooler and, therefore, visually recede; the yellow-greens are warmer, popping out and seeming to be closer than they really are. At the extremes of variation are gray-leaved plants (among them *Santolina chamaecyparissus* and *Stachys byzantina*) and those with golden foliage (*Lysimachia nummularia* 'Aurea' and *Hosta* 'Piedmont Gold'); there are also plants with reddish or purple leaves (*Sedum* 'Rosy Glow', *Heuchera micrantha* 'Palace Purple' and *Ajuga reptans* 'Burgundy Glow').

All too often, red- and purple-leaved plants are overlooked in planning a garden, and much is lost in the way of creative potential. For this reason, such genera as *Caladium, Begonia, Heuchera, Sedum, Bergenia, Epimedium, Astilbe, Ajuga, Fittonia* and *Ophiopogon*—just a sampling of the ones that contain purple- or red-leaved species suited to use as groundcovers—should be given careful consideration. Sometimes, this feature is offered up only at the start or end of the season, for example, the way the fronds of certain ferns unfurl with a pink-bronze cast before turning green (*Dryopteris erythrosora* or Autumn fern), or the way other plants such as (Parthenocissus species (Boston ivy and Virginia creeper) turn color only at season's end (see "Autumn Color").

The texture of a leaf—puckered or fluted, crinkled or pleated—and whether it has a coat of silvery hairs as does lamb's ears (*Stachys byzantina*) or wine-colored hairs in the case of certain begonias, can alter how we see the underlying color, whether it be green or otherwise. All of these features that look like mere window dressing to the human eye are really botanical adaptations with important biological functions, usually related to a plant's use of moisture and sunlight or its need to attract or repel particular insects and other creatures.

Generally speaking, hairy leaves help a plant to conserve moisture, deter insect pests and shade the leaf surface by mediating the amount of light that hits it. They are harder to chew on, so caterpillars are hindered from feasting on them, and even some pesky animals seem to dislike their texture as a foodstuff. To the gardener's eye, these features are frequently what make one plant appear more beautiful than another, but it is important to remember that they offer clues about the plant's heritage and, therefore, its use in

Hosta *'Kabitan', shown with* Galium, *is one of many hostas whose golden leaves warm up a planting.*

the landscape. Fuzzy, silver-leaved plants are generally drought tolerant, for instance, and prefer full sun.

THE GIFT OF VARIEGATION

Variegation, the genetically inherited irregular pattern of color in a leaf (or petal), is a quality many gardeners come to recognize as perhaps the most useful of all in creating exciting planting designs. In addition to their sheer beauty, variegated plants with areas of white, gold or red in the foliage seem to "pop" out of, or advance visually in, the garden. This is especially useful in brightening dark spots, as in a woodland garden or under tall trees, where the light-colored leaf portions make it look as though shafts of sunlight had penetrated the canopy to shine on them alone. In shade gardens in particular, variegated plants play a key role in creating highlights, making things look not so dim after all. Some of the best gardeners I know are variegation addicts. They search out—in mail-order catalogs, at rare-plant nurseries and even by begging cuttings from curators of public-garden collections—unusually marked forms of plants.

When I started gardening, I would have shuddered to think of planting several variegated or otherwise oddly colored foliage plants together. Now I can't *shake* the image of a small patch in a friend's Massachusetts garden, I liked it so much; it combines bloodgrass (*Imperata cylindrica rubra*), striped red and green, golden feather fe-

*Chameleon plant (*Houttuynia cordata*) and golden feverfew (*Chrysanthemum Parthenium 'Aureum'*) in the Massachusetts garden of Bob Zeleniak and John Trexler.*

verfew (*Chrysanthemum parthenium* 'Aureum') and the chameleon plant (*Houttuynia cordata*), splotched with red, pink, green and cream. In another garden I admire, behind an inner-city apartment building, there is another dramatic tapestry: Yellow-and-green-striped *Yucca filamentosa* 'Golden Sword' plays off *Liriope muscari* 'Silvery Sunproof' (its stripes creamy yellow and white). Nearby, two lungworts, each with a different pattern of silvery spots (and a slightly different leaf shape as an added, although subtle, twist) are planted beside each other for maximum impact. *Pulmonaria saccharata* 'Janet Fisk' and *P. s.* 'Roy Davidson' have never looked so good to me, and now they are growing as a happy couple in my own garden, too. A garden-writer friend takes his own liberties with variegation. Beneath a wave of green-and-white-striped manna grass (*Glyceria aquatica* 'Variegata'), the variegated goutweed (*Aegopodium podograria* 'Variegatum') forms a wild carpet. To top it off, he planted the very flashy

(although sadly overlooked) perennial *Tovara virginiana*, sometimes listed as a polygonum.

These daring plant combinations work because the larger gardens around them have enough solid-color stabilizing elements to lend support, in the form of plants, stone and even mulch materials. The mixed variegates represent a small portion of the total design, a few brilliant pockets. A whole garden of variegated plants would be as disastrous as one without any at all.

If the look of mixed variegations makes you uncomfortable, go easy on it. Perhaps using a single variegated species is enough to break up the monotony and any more would be too much. I do believe that at least a small accent area of such lively blends can make a good garden a great one, but you may disagree. And your own take on these combinations is what's important—your garden is your personal art. If the effect is like an M. C. Escher optical-illusion print and you just can't seem to focus, tone things down until you're happy with the image.

Another plus about variegates: Sometimes the green form of a

plant is highly invasive; such is the case with goutweed (*Aegopodium Podagraria*), for instance. The variegated form, however, is fast-covering without being impossible to control; prune the roots regularly with a garden spade to stay within the bounds allotted, and you will keep the upper hand. This reduced vigor among variegates results from the smaller areas of green tissue for food production (in white or yellow areas, no photosynthesis can occur, so less food can be made).

In many cases this means the variegated form will be slower to propagate and thus more expensive to purchase. But anyone who has had a look at a bed of variegated *Pachysandra terminalis* or *Vinca minor* will probably never be satisfied with the plain green again and will ante up for at least a small amount to break up those formerly all-green masses.

Occasionally, variegates will send up shoots that are all green. Cut off these "reversions," as they are called, because they tend to be more energetic and can eventually overcome the more desirable, although slower growing, form.

The green-and-white foliage of Miscanthus sinensis *'Variegatus' and a variegated dogwood (background) play off one another.*

LOOKING AT LEAF FORMS

In creating your own living mosaics, contrasts of leaf form improve the picture just as contrasts of color do. Juxtaposing spiky foliage plants (*Iris cristata*, for example) with feathery ones (ferns or astilbes, for instance) with others that have big, bold leaves (hostas and *Bergenia*, to

name two) greatly increases the impact of each. A planting of Siberian iris, yucca and ornamental grasses would be monotonous—spikes, spikes and more spikes. But add a few wisely placed variants—big groupings of bold-leaved *Hosta plantaginea* (the hosta that can take sun best), or ornamental rhubarb (*Rheum palmatum*), and a swath of relatively sun-tolerant ferns such as ostrich (*Matteuccia pensylvanica*) or hay-scented (*Dennstaedtia punctilobula*), or maybe some artemisia for a similarly ferny effect—and the picture starts to improve.

Sometimes, the similarity of leaf form can be just what you're looking for, a kind of subtle statement of same but different. A mixed planting of ferns, for instance, brings into sharp focus just how different these similar plants are. Rhododen-

dron, Japanese holly (*Ilex crenata*) and the low groundcover wintergreen (*Gaultheria procumbens*) all have similarly shaped, evergreen leaves of leathery substance, but they range from about 6 inches long in the case of a large rhodie to around an inch in the wintergreen and half that or less in the *Ilex crenata*. Heath (*Erica*), heather (*Calluna*) and prostrate juniper make another effective same-but-different trio. So, have a good close look at leaf color, texture, shape and size before you let the charm of flowers steal all your attention.

Designer Kim Hawks of Niche Gardens, Chapel Hill, North Carolina, punctuates a mat of Rubus calycinoides *with* Carex phyllocephala 'Sparkler'.

Contrasting foliar forms—straplike daylilies, the compound leaves of goutweed and large ones of bergenia—improves each.

SAY IT WITH FLOWERS

As we have said, flowers are a relatively ephemeral component of the garden picture. That doesn't mean they are to be discounted, but when planning a groundcover planting, they are rarely the first order of priority. Ferns, because of their primitive physiology, don't produce flowers at all; does that mean they would not make an attractive choice of groundcover? The fact that a hosta produces flowers is a bonus; with or without the flowers, hosta is a fine choice, particularly in shade gardens. Some gardeners, preferring the leaves alone, even cut the hostas' flower stalks off as they emerge, particularly those of the *Hosta sieboldiana* varieties, which barely clear the top of the foliage. Similarly, the flowers of lamb's ears are removed in many gardens to leave just the fuzzy silver mats of leaves, although I think that's wasting an aspect of the plant, in both cases.

Nurseries know only too well that plants sell best when they are in flower, however fleeting a time that may be. Too many gardeners who seek out the pink-flowering form of a certain plant over the white or the cultivar with the biggest double flowers have no idea what color the same plant's foliage turns in fall, or whether it produces fruit or seed heads for late-season interest. A number of the low-growing shrubs suitable for groundcovering (*Cotoneaster*, *Ilex* and *Euonymous*, for instance) produce colorful, long-lasting berries, as do wintergreen (*Gaultheria procumbens*) and partridgeberry (*Mitchella repens*). Astilbe flowers look great left right in place to dry naturally; so do those of some *Sedum*, notably *S. spectabile* 'Autumn Joy'. Even the plainest green form of Japanese barberry is a gem in the fall, when it goes through various hot shades of orange, red and purple and

Groundcovers for Damp Spots

Acorus gramineus (Japanese sweet flag)

Andromeda polifolia (bog rosemary)

Caltha palustris (marsh marigold)

Cardamine species (cardamine)

Hedyotis or *Houstonia caerulea* (bluets)

Houttuynia cordata (chameleon plant)

Lysimachia nummularia (moneywort)

Matteuccia Struthiopteris pensylvanica (ostrich fern)

Mentha pulegium (pennyroyal)

Osmunda claytoniana (interrupted fern)

Sarracenia species (pitcherplant)

Impatiens nestles among the foliage and flowers of hostas.

has fire-engine—red berries, too. Hostas, although rarely grown for this reason, turn a lovely yellow before going dormant.

Planning to create a continuous season of bloom and to avoid flower color clashes is easier when massing groundcovers than in designing the conventional flower or shrub garden, as usually fewer species of plants are in question. That doesn't mean it's foolproof. Be sure *before* you plant that you really want the purple-flowered vinca under that rhododendron with the different hue of purple flowers. Nature is very forgiving when it comes to color combinations—orange and purple are great together and even some reds with pink— but certain near misses (two difficult shades of the same color, for example) may be a bit too jarring for many tastes. The white form of the vinca is a safer way out, if you're uncertain.

Sometimes the attribute of long-lasting flowers makes a groundcover particularly valuable. *Vinca minor*, sweet alyssum, verbena, *Potentilla*, green and gold (*Chrysogonum virginianum*) or a rose such as *Rosa* 'The Fairy' are examples of potential groundcovers whose flowers are borne over a very long season. In these cases, more attention must be paid to flower color because they promise to stick around. 'The Fairy', for instance, can get a bit close to Pepto-Bismol™ pink for some spots in the garden.

Groundcovers for Late-Season Color

FLOWERS

Anemone ×hybrida (Japanese anemone)
Aster ×frikartii, *A. novae-angliae* 'Purple Dome' (aster)
Ceratostigma plumbaginoides (leadwort; foliage also colorful)
Chrysanthemum species (chrysanthemum)
Cyclamen species (hardy cyclamen)
Dahlia species (dahlia)
Eupatorium coelestinum (hardy ageratum)
Ornamental grasses
Sedum spectabile 'Autumn Joy' (Autumn Joy sedum)
Solidago sphacelata 'Golden Fleece' (dwarf goldenrod)

FOLIAGE

Arctostaphylos uva-ursi (bearberry)
Cyclamen species (hardy cyclamen)
Dryopteris erythrosora (Japanese autumn fern)
Hosta species (hosta; turns yellow in fall)
Juniperus horizontalis 'Douglasii' (Waukegan juniper)
Microbiota decussata (Siberian carpet cypress)
Nandina domestica (heavenly bamboo)
Parthenocissus species (Boston ivy, Virginia creeper)
Paxistima canbyi (paxistima)
Rubus calycinoides (flowering raspberry)
Stephanandra incisa (cut-leaf stephanandra)
Vaccinium species (blueberry)
Xanthorhiza simplicissima (yellowroot)

THINKING THINGS THROUGH

Where do you want a groundcover, or combination of groundcovers? Sometimes the decision is prompted by the desire to solve a problem, such as the ones we discussed in Chapter 1—to hold a bank, to cover spots where grass won't grow or you can't mow and so on. These are straightforward cases; the conditions dictate where you will plant. When the motivation is more aesthetic or prompted by a general desire to reduce high-maintenance areas of the lawn and garden, there's room for more creativity. Many times, you can select a spot depending on which groundcovers you'd like to grow.

In either situation—unless yours is the most formal of landscapes—avoid a monotonous approach. Don't till a perfect 6-foot circle around every last tree and plant it with mirror-image arrangements of daffodils and ivy. Generally speaking, amoebic shapes are better

choices. (You can "draw" on the existing sod or ground with a sprinkling of powdered limestone or use your garden hose to create temporary outlines.) And consider leaving the area under a tree or two just as it is.

Now is the time to ask yourself how much lawn you really need. Though most Americans cling to their lawns as though they were symbols of democracy, all that grass is actually more of an albatross than they realize. A small area of turf grass is a delight—for volleyball or picnics or as a green oasis just to look at—and should be part of all but the most confined landscape designs. But any

more than you will actually use is simply a waste of the energy (both yours and the gas or electricity to run the mower), the chemicals and the water it requires to sustain it.

Island beds cut out of the lawn can be geometric or freeform; the choice is yours and depends on what you plan to plant, and the shape of the property and existing elements. Remember, even if the hard lines of a rectangular or square bed are best for your site, the bed needn't be planted stiffly. The contrast of formal structure and effusive planting (think of all those vast English perennial borders) can make a winner.

BEFORE YOU SHOP . . .

Conventional gardening wisdom, the stuff of most horticultural texts and garden-club lectures, says always to plan on paper. For many gardeners, particularly those getting started in the art of landscaping, this is good advice. But for some who are more inclined to seat-of-the-pants bursts of creativity—you probably know who you are—groundcovers are a pretty safe place to try your garden designing freehand, because a typical planting will involve only a few species. Some of our greatest garden designers work on intuition, roughing out a basic plan and then improvising a bit on the spot at planting time. And all of them know to watch the garden evolve, to take cues from what comes up rather than from what they drew.

When planning a groundcover planting, particularly of a large

area, it is more important to do quantity calculations on paper than to create an actual design. How many plants do you need to fill the space? First, you must know the recommended spacing of the plant or plants you intend to use. Frequently a range such as "18 to 24 inches" is given to express the spread of mature plants (what we use to determine approximate spacing). Most plants reach this "mature" spread in about three years, or some in as many as five, so that is how long the planting will require to fill in. For faster coverage, use the lower number or a tighter spacing, perhaps twice as close, but be sure to note what spacing you are working with when you make your calculations so that you can use it in planting, too.

If a plant is to be allowed a

square foot of space, and you have a 10-foot square to plant, it is easy to calculate that you'd need about 100 plants. Determining this can be puzzling when the shape of the bed is circular or irregular, though. Here is the formula used for all bedding schemes by Michael A. Ruggiero, senior garden curator at the New York Botanical Garden.

1. Determine the number of square feet in the area to be planted.

For **rectangles** and **squares**, multiply length times width.

For **circles**, multiply the radius of the circle by itself and then multiply the total by *pi* (3.1416).

For **ovals**, multiply the average radius by itself and then multiply the total by pi (3.1416).

For **triangles**, multiply one-half the height by the base.

2. Determine the number of square inches in the area to be planted by multiplying the number of square feet determined in Step 1 by 144 (the number of inches in a square foot).

3. Determine the number of square inches a mature plant will cover by multiplying the number of inches of suggested spacing between plants by itself.

4. Divide the number of square inches required for one plant into the number of square inches in the plot. The number will be the total plants needed for that plot.

Further details of planting your groundcovers are provided in Chapter 3.

Make Mine a Meadow?

Is a meadow for everyone, as purveyors of the "instant" canned mixes seem to proclaim? Hardly, although meadow gardening with native grasses and wildflowers deserves consideration by those wishing to cover some ground (even if a "minimeadow" might be more to the point). To create a real meadow, you need land; otherwise, the traditional plant combinations will be out of scale. Six-foot-tall grasses and flowers, typical in a Midwestern prairie, are simply too big for the average backyard.

In the limited space of the New York Botanical Garden Native Plant Garden, for instance, the designer utilized grasses such as *Andropogon virginicus*, *Uniola latifolia*, *Sporobolus heterolepsis* and *Panicum virgatum* in one area together with the wildflowers butterfly weed *(Asclepias)*, New England asters *(Aster novae-angliae)*, coreopsis *(Coreopsis verticillata)*, purple coneflower *(Echinacea purpurea)*, the exceptionally long-blooming rough false sunflower *(Heliopsis helanthoides)*, downy skullcap *(Scutellaria incana)*, blazing star *(Liatris)* and brown-eyed Susan *(Rudbeckia triloba)*. Smaller combinations of some of these plants might appeal to homeowners considering a naturalistic flower bed or border.

A caveat: Meadow gardening is a way to cover a lot of ground,

The marsh marigold (Caltha palustris) *is a good choice for wet spots.*

Low-growing roses make good groundcovers, and will cascade gracefully over walls.

A Rose Is a Rose Is a Groundcover

Try these roses that are well adapted to covering the ground:

Meidiland landscape roses
'Red Cascade' (miniature rose)
Rosa × 'Max Graf'
Rosa rugosa alba (white rugosa rose)
Rosa × 'Sea Foam' (shrub rose)

Rosa × 'Simplicity' (hedge rose)
Rosa × 'The Fairy' (hybrid *Polyantha* shrub rose)
Rosa × wichuraiana (memorial rose)
Rosa wichuraiana 'New Dawn' (ever-blooming hybrid)

but it is not accomplished by simply throwing out your mower and letting your lawn grow in. Usually, all that will yield is neighbors' complaints. Shaking some canned seed mix into the mess won't improve things much, either. Many mixes are blends containing high percentages of showy annuals, for a fast burst of color. What a meadow relies on is a balanced community of compatible perennial flowers and grasses.

Better to clear the site completely (see the section on site preparation, page 32) and start with a high-quality mix of perennial flowers and grasses appropriate to your locale. These will take three to five years to come into their own, and meanwhile you'll have to keep undesirable weeds out. Best bet: Start by plugging year-old perennial plants into your cleared area. They will start blooming from the first season on and get the jump on many weeds.

3

GROUNDCOVER PLANTING AND GROWING GUIDE

LEAVE NO STONE UNTURNED

Gertrude Jekyll, the revered English gardener of the Edwardian era, told a revealing story about soil preparation in her book *Wood and Garden*. Certain visitors to her garden at Munstead Wood, where the soil was naturally shallow and poor, had expressed the notion that Miss Jekyll must possess some magical touch with plants or that the soil wasn't really as bad as she claimed it to be. Spying a particularly robust *Lilium giganteum* growing 10 feet tall in an unlikely spot, one such doubting visitor again expressed suspicion that the soil wasn't meager at all.

Rather than waste her breath arguing otherwise, Miss Jekyll just kept walking, right in the direction of a 12-foot-wide by 4-foot-deep excavation a little farther on in the woodland.

"Why are you making all this mess in your pretty wood?" the visitor asked. "Are you quarrying stone, or is it for the cellar of a building?"

"I only wanted to plant a few more of those big Lilies," a triumphant Miss Jekyll replied, "and you see in my soil they would not have a chance unless the ground was thoroughly prepared. . . ."

Proper soil preparation is the basis of sound gardening, whatever it is that you wish to grow. Perhaps the most common mistake made by beginning gardeners (and many experienced but lazy gardeners who ought to know better) is that soil is soil. One can't simply walk about the yard looking for an open spot of ground, open it up and insert a plant.

Besides ensuring that plants have a chance to root well, receive proper nourishment and adequate though not prolonged exposure to moisture, well-prepared soil is also the first line of defense against the possibility of damage from disease and insect infestation. A healthy soil produces healthy plants like nothing else can—no quick-fix chemical fertilizer, fungicide or pesticide applied before or after the fact. (For more on how soil preparation and other cultural practices combine into an environmentally sound form of horticultural preventive medicine called "integrated pest management," see Chapter 5). Groundcovers are principally intended to be long-term aspects of the landscape, so building your soil up before planting is particularly important for maximum return.

Wildflowers, including a lilac-colored patch of phlox, form a vibrant springtime carpet under a canopy of dogwoods.

Clay soil

Sandy soil

Loamy soil

A few incredibly determined creatures—some would call them monsters—like kudzu don't seem to care where you plant them, but most plants you will wish to cultivate will more than pay you back in kind, according to the quality of welcome mat you put out for them. If you are stingy with the organic amendments, most plants will hold out for more (for a list of groundcovers suited to poor, dry soils, see page 90).

First, determine the quality of the topsoil— the uppermost layer of the earth, typically organic in composition—that you have to work with. Dig down with a spade or trowel and see how deep it is. At what point do you reach significant resistance? A good garden soil is workable down at least 8 inches, although just preparing it once and forgetting it in years to come will quickly see those 8 inches eroded by weather and sapped of vigor by hungry plants. Serious gardeners work hard, season after season, to replenish and even further build the soil, so that it is a good shovel-head or more deep and able to hold moisture long enough for plants to get a good drink, but not long enough for water to stand in it and promote problems.

Next, determine the basic structure of your soil. Pick up a handful of damp earth and squeeze it in your hand. If the mass holds together and stays that way, you probably have a clay soil. Stickiness is a sign of clay, a fine-particled medium that tends to form long-lasting clods and drains poorly. To test further for clay, dig out a shallow depression about a foot across (a couple of inches deep is plenty) and fill it with water. Observe the time it takes for the water to seep into the soil below. If it's more than an hour, your soil is probably clay. You may have noticed pooling in the garden after a hard rain.

Back to the squeeze test. If the moist soil forms a mass when squeezed and then slowly crumbles apart when you open your hand and flick it with a finger, what you probably have is loam. Loam, the most desirable soil for gardening because it is a good blend of clay and sand, typically contains plenty of decomposed organic matter, or humus, so that it is fertile and well draining.

If you have a sandy soil, it won't form a mass at all when squeezed, but will spill through your fingers instead. Sandy soils are often more tan in color than soils of a more organic type (those that are humus rich and made up of broken-down organic materials like old plant parts and decayed manure). Sand is actually tiny particles of rock, so it does not have the capacity to absorb moisture. A sandy soil is very fast draining, often to a fault, as very little or nothing is soaked up to be available to roots later. Most soils are not precisely one type or the other, so it is possible and in fact common to have a clayey loam or a sandy loam, for example. The best soils are actually blends.

Generally speaking, it's best to stay out of the garden when the soil is wet; even a good soil will suffer from being worked when waterlogged. Clay soils, which have very little air space between the particles anyway, are particularly susceptible to damage from being compacted when wet. In spring, and any time there is heavy rain, wait until what is called the chocolate-cake stage or crumb stage to get going in the garden. A soil is in this condition when a small amount of it rubbed gently between the thumb and fingers does not stick into a paste but crumbles, like a properly moist but not undercooked piece of chocolate cake.

PREPARING THE SITE

Is there something currently growing where you want to install a groundcover planting? More often than not, the area being converted to groundcover is currently cultivated as a grass lawn or perhaps a weedy patch of earth. Although it will require some work to remove weeds before installing your groundcover plants, this step cannot be skipped nor any shortcuts be taken.

Weeds have traditionally been eliminated through the use of chemical herbicides, but environmentally conscious gardeners should stick with safer methods of mechanical removal, as even the latest, less-toxic herbicides on the market may prove to have deleterious effects. Remember, no one knew that DDT would prove deadly when it was hailed as a miracle invention. It's wiser to adopt a better-safe-than-sorry approach to gardening than risk any further harm to the environment, ourselves and other living creatures. Besides, mechanical removal usually boils down to a little hard work, and who can't use the benefit of some exercise? Non-chemical ways you can eliminate weeds include the following:

SMOTHER THEM WITH PLASTIC.

If you are not in a hurry to plant, cover the area to be weeded with a sheet of heavy, opaque plastic (black is ideal, but a poly tarp can also be used), weighed down at the edges with soil or stones. Leave in place for at least an entire growing season; the longer the better. The high temperatures beneath the mulch and the light deprivation combine to cook the weeds to death. Remove the plastic, then turn or till soil, removing dead plant debris with a rake and by hand-sifting.

A shorter-term solution, called soil solarization, calls for covering the ground with clear plastic for a month during hot, sunny weather. You must dig out all plants growing in the area first, and start with open soil. The clear plastic creates sufficient heat to kill both weed seeds and also most soilborne diseases, effectively sterilizing the soil; a downside is that it effectively kills even "friendly" creatures in the uppermost layer,

too. Soil is not mere dirt; it is a living organism, a complex community of insects, bacteria and other microorganisms that make it possible for plants to draw life from it. Over time, these beneficials will creep back in from adjacent areas of the garden, and the soil will be restored to optimum health.

MULCH THEM WITH NEWSPAPER.

Spread multiple thicknesses of black-and-white newsprint over the area to be reclaimed, overlapping the paper and weighing it down with stones. If you desire it for aesthetic reasons, cover with mulch such as bark chips. Without light, and unable to penetrate the paper and mulch, many weed plants below the surface will die in about a year or at least be thwarted. To plant groundcovers in this spot, do not remove the mulch and paper (the paper will eventually decompose); simply slit *X*'s big enough to let some water seep through into the mulch at the appropriate spacing for each plant and insert young plants into the openings. If the newsprint is laid in spring, you can begin planting in fall; or paper in fall and plant the following spring.

DIG THEM OUT.

Want to plant next week, or even tomorrow? Get out your shovel, hoe and tiller, plus a rake for sifting through the mess of weeds,

rocks and soil, then get to work. Don't just skim the stuff at surface level; really dig in. This method is cheap, effective—and hard work. A hand mattock, like a small pick and hoe combination, will prove invaluable for wrestling tap-rooted weeds such as dock out of the ground. Weed seeds may resprout, but use of mulch after the area is replanted will help suppress them.

LIFT SOD.

When large areas of turf are to be removed, it may be fastest and easiest to rent a sod-cutting machine, or hire a lawn service that owns one to do the work for you. Sod cutters do this job quickly and neatly, leaving clean edges and digging up only a minimum of the topsoil compared with digging the turf up with a shovel. Lifted sod makes great compost in time, so be sure to keep the stuff and add it to your heap.

BURN.

In some areas, controlled burning is permitted to clear land of brush and troublesome weeds and weed seeds. Fire can be a helpful, natural way to weed out undesirables and promote other plants; restoration work in some habitats such as the Midwestern prairie relies heavily on yearly burning. Ask your local cooperative extension agent about the feasibility and the fire department about the legality of burning in your specific situation and site.

SOIL IMPROVEMENT

Once the area is basically weed free (the population of rocks will have been diminished in the process, too), soil improvement is next on the agenda. I have a basic rule, hammered into my oftentimes-lazy consciousness by a gardening friend I work with regularly: Never open up the soil for any reason without tucking in some organic matter while you're at it.

This means that any time a plant is removed or replaced, bulbs are planted, the garden is cultivated or a whole new area is prepped for planting, texture-improving elements like peat moss, leaf mold or other composted material should be incorporated. (I frequently add sand, too, in small amounts, but sand is inorganic—helpful for drainage but useless for improving moisture retention.)

Do not skimp. Your soil and, therefore, your plants will thank you. And instead of watching the level of the beds get lower and lower each passing year due to depletion by erosion and plants' appetites, you will see garden beds actually get fluffier and more raised as time goes by. Your soil will be deeper —better for good root growth —and drainage will improve. A well-tended soil is a precious resource.

When starting a new garden, I like to spread an inch or two of sand on top of the weeded area, and a 3-inch layer of peat moss on top of that, then dig the layers in shovelful by shovelful until the whole thing is well mixed. This usually takes turning the bed twice; I like to know that my soil is at least the depth of the head of my long-handled shovel, about a foot. After mixing, rake the surface level. My own garden soil is deep and loamy naturally; if it were extremely clayey or sandy, I would turn in even more liberal amounts of organic matter, perhaps several inches of rotted manure along with several of peat moss.

Many gardeners regularly apply lime to new plantings (to "sweeten" the soil, which raises the pH to a less acidic level), or to lawns annually. Similarly, they sprinkle soil-acidifying materials such as aluminum sulfate or better yet, cottonseed meal (an organic soil acidifier, preferable to chemical materials) where they wish to grow acid-loving plants. This is not recommended as a regular practice; it is too haphazard, too imprecise. Do not attempt to amend soil pH unless you have it tested first. The local cooperative extension usually will perform pH tests and tell you if you need to lime and, if so, how much to apply per square foot.

PLANTING PATTERNS

Although I frequently eyeball the spacing of plants in a small- or medium-size area, when working on a large scale it is best to plan more precisely for even coverage. I like to imagine the ground as if it were imprinted with a grid pattern, like graph paper, the scale of which is the correct spacing between the plants in question. I place one plant at the center point of each imaginary box; a similar effect will be achieved by placing one plant in each corner of every box on the grid.

An easy way to create rough guidelines for your grid is to work with an appropriate length of heavy string attached to a spike at either end, the kind of device used by vegetable gardeners planting long rows of seeds to keep the row straight. Say you are working with plants that are to be spaced every 18 inches. Stretch the string from end to end of the planting area, inserting the stakes into the soil at either boundary, then plant one plant under it every 18 inches (you can mark the cord with bits of colored tape every 18 inches to eliminate the need to measure each time). When you finish one row, move the stakes back 18 inches and repeat the process. Continue until the bed is planted.

I frequently place the young plants on the ground without actually digging them in until I have finished spacing all of them out. This gives me a chance to look at the rough layout before committing to it, which is particularly helpful when it is a mix of several varieties. I stand back and look at the areas of each particular plant and try to imagine them grown in. If you do decide simply to lay the plants on the soil surface and then go back and plant them, don't do this at high noon in July; work in the late afternoon or sometime on a cloudy, damp day, so the plants don't get cooked before they're in the ground. Or dig plants in as you go, if you prefer.

Once the plants are in place, they need to be watered in well.

This first drink is the most important one of the plant's life, because transplanting is a major stress. Don't underestimate the importance of this step. Water slowly and deeply for best results. Special preparation should be made to permit water to have time to permeate before running off when planting on a slope. When planting a mass of larger, woody shrubs, it may be wise to create a small dish of earth around each one and trickle water into the dish slowly, plant by plant, rather than watering the entire area, much of which will not have any roots in it at all yet.

When watering, think of which kind of rainstorm really helps the garden most. A quick downpour does little more than pelt the plants and soil into a sorry mess, and much of the water then runs off in a true case of adding insult to injury. A slow, steady drizzle over many hours is always the most beneficial, because the water has time to percolate gradually into the soil, so if you're using overhead sprinklers, keep this in mind.

The least wasteful method of watering, particularly in hot weather when the evaporation rate is high during sprinkling, is achieved at ground level via drip irrigation or soaker hoses. If you do not have such a system, which can be installed quite cheaply by do-it-yourselfers, sprinkling is fine. But remember, don't just shoot a jet of water at each plant. All you'll do is dislodge it, and the roots will still be thirsting for water.

STAY AHEAD OF WEEDS

Once an area is planted, the greatest challenge will be keeping weeds from overtaking young groundcovers. A garden without a gardener is a jungle waiting to happen. More than a few gardens are lost to weeds every year; it simply isn't enough to do the planting, you have to do the weeding, too. Postplanting weed control is essential the first couple of years in particular, until desirables fill in.

To lessen the load, apply several inches of an organic mulch such as shredded bark, wood chips, pine needles or partially rotted leaves to help suppress weeds and weed seeds. Fine-textured, lightweight organic mulches such as cocoa or buckwheat hulls, shredded stable bedding (finely ground woodchips used to absorb wastes in stalls) and even rotted leaves and pine needles will gradually become part of the topsoil as they continue to decompose. This is good for soil building, but in cases where groundcovers will take several years to fill in, a somewhat heavier weight of mulch may be preferable, as it will not have to be replenished so often to remain somewhat impenetrable.

Some gardeners like to use annual foliage plants like coleuses or polka-dot plants, or annual flowers like impatiens and begonias, to fill in the gaps until the permanent plants thicken up. Use care in selecting your annual fillers, though, or be careful to deadhead regularly. Some are vigorous self-sowers, and you'll have them in years to come if they are allowed to go to seed.

Planting in fall can also help gardeners stay ahead of many weeds that are geared to germinate in spring; by the time they do, your groundcovers will already have had a head start. And fall can be a sensible planting time for other reasons. Generally speaking, the moister, cooler weather of autumn means you'll have less watering to do and fewer stressed-out transplants to contend with.

AN OUNCE OF AFTERCARE

Once a groundcover planting begins to settle in and mature, it will (generally speaking) demand less and less of the gardener's time. Fewer weeds will penetrate, and most older plants need less watering than those just getting started, because their root systems are better developed. Groundcovers aren't carefree, however. Here is what you can expect to do as a minimum to keep plantings in peak condition.

DEADHEADING. Deadheading, that is, removing the flowers as they go by, will frequently result in a second, although usu-

Remove spent blossoms to prolong bloom and prevent the formation of seeds. That way, flowers devote more of their energy to blooming.

ally less showy, bloom. *Tiarella*, for instance, and the perennial geraniums appreciate deadheading, among others. Self-cleaning flowering plants—those whose faded flowers seem to remove themselves—are the exception, but they make good choices when what you want is an easy-care groundcover. Impatiens' flowers seem to just disappear, and more follow as if by magic. The same is true with *Vinca minor*. Daylilies, on the other hand, are the opposite: Their spent blossoms, produced daily, hang on the scapes like so many wet tissues. From a distance, a mass planting of daylilies looks great even without a gardener's daily round of cleanup; up close, the picture may not be so pretty. Take this into account, or plan to devote the time required or select something naturally tidier.

HAIRCUTS. Many groundcovers appreciate an occasional haircut. Certain flowering perennials, in particular, tend to get leggy or floppy by midsummer unless they are whacked back after bloom. Plants that respond well to this treatment include the hybrid perennial geraniums 'Johnson's Blue' and 'Wargrave Pink', catmint (*Nepeta mussinii*), and lady's-mantle (*Alchemilla mollis*), which can also simply be selectively cleaned up by removing the oldest leaves. Most artemisias should be cut back at midsummer to look good again later.

Certain evergreen to semi-evergreen herbaceous plants prefer their trims to remove damaged foliage in late winter. Hellebores, for instance, will push up lots of fresh green growth if

cut back at that time. *Bergenia* may benefit from some tidying up, as will a *Lamium* with persistent foliage and *Liriope* in areas where it is marginally hardy, among others.

My general rule: If a non-woody plant looks battered by winter, bugs or slugs or is flopping over messily from too much top growth, try giving it a trim. You've got nothing to lose, and you will probably get fresh leaves and perhaps even another flush of flowers later on.

DIVISION. Herbaceous perennial plants need to be divided less frequently when groundcovering is the desired effect than they do in a traditional garden situation. Dense coverage is exactly what you want. However, sometimes flowering may diminish, signaling it's time for dividing, or the centers of each plant within a grouping may die out. Best to plan in advance for such eventualities, particularly in large-scale plantings. Do you really want to divide 1,000 square feet of plants every three years, or would it be wiser to choose another plant altogether in the first place, one that doesn't suffer when it grows together thickly?

Sometimes, you will choose to divide not because the plants need it so much but because you need the plants for another area of the garden. Most spring-flowering plants should be divided in fall and late summer, and fall bloomers in spring (this helps you avoid interference with flowering). Rugged individuals such as daylilies and irises can be divided after blooming, even in the heat of summer. In many

cases, it is easiest to divide plants when dormant (early spring or late fall), but don't wait too long in the fall with marginally hardy ones.

There is no more mystery to the task of division than there is to cutting up a sandwich to share with friends. In each case, everybody wants a little piece of everything, not just a bit of the bread without any cheese, or some foliage without roots attached. Refer to the illustrations on page 37 for some examples of division.

There are other methods besides dividing for increasing your stock of plants. Herbaceous plants are also frequently increased by seed as well as by cuttings, usually pieces of stem with leaves attached, as outlined in the *Perennials* book in this series. This is similar to the method used to increase shrubs and woody vines detailed on page 39; few woody plants are increased by division

FEEDING. If all goes according to plan, it will be hard to get between individual plants to cultivate once they have filled in. Instead of struggling to scratch in fertilizer for each and every plant, top-dress the whole bed in late winter or early spring when plants are still dormant, by applying a 2-inch layer of rotted manure or the prescribed amount of an all-natural organic fertilizer (products containing such substances as bone and blood meal, for example) called for on the package label.

MULCHING. All groundcovers need mulching when first planted, as discussed. Eventually, groundcovers form a living mulch, but a little bit of the organic kind layered on the soil surface each fall is beneficial. Even where mulch isn't essential to prevent heaving during repeated thaws or to check erosion, organic mulches such as composted stable bedding, shredded leaves or bark and others eventually break down into the soil and help improve it. Plants that specifically require a mulch, particularly in the northern extremes of their hardiness range, are so noted in Chapter 4. In the best of years, nature mulches the ground each winter with a blanket of snow.

When digging up a plant (here, a hosta), get as large a root ball as possible.

Use a sharp knife to divide the root ball in half or quarters.

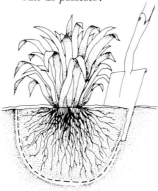
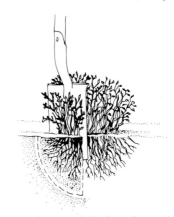

Above, from left to right: *The roots rarely exceed the boundaries described by the foliage above them. Some perennials, such as astilbe, can be divided by removing only a section of the plant and leaving the rest in the ground. After digging up daylilies, divide them by thrusting two pitchforks into the roots and pulling the tubers apart.*

Miscanthus sinensis
'Gracillimus' in snow

WHEN YOUR GROUNDCOVER IS A LAWN

A bit of lawn is fine, well suited to high-traffic recreation areas.

Although the portion of the typical American yard devoted to grass appears to be on the decline, owing to increased awareness about chemical pesticides and fertilizers, the reality of limited water resources and other environmental factors, there will always be some who wish to maintain an area of turf grass. Not so far in the future, an evergreen lawn will be possible in many areas of North America, according to researchers at the National Agricultural Research Center in Beltsville, Maryland.

The lawn of the future will be a combination of zoysia, a warm-weather grass that goes brown in the cold, and tall fescue, which displays greater cold tolerance and is, therefore, green when zoysia isn't. Neither is particularly fussy about water, fertilizer or even mowing, so perhaps this new superlawn will be environmentally sound and easy-care, too. For now, though, most of us are growing grasses that are anything but.

The way America mows its lawn isn't mere horticulture. It's economics and politics, too. If you find yourself behind the mower, you're in a position to vote for a healthier environment. Traditional lawn-care regimes—applying chemical nutrients to feed the grass and raking up the grass clippings for disposal—are outdated, wasteful and environmentally damaging, according to experts, many of whom are promoting a message of "don't bag it" as an alternative. Equally disastrous is bagging or even burning fallen leaves, which thankfully has been reduced by many municipalities as the implementation of recycl-

William John Wallis, a New Jersey landscape architect, creates a sunken circle of Pachysandra *to contrast angular lines of house and deck and limit lawn area.*

A more traditional lawn, but one reduced by the installation of a shrub island in background.

ing programs has begun to turn the stuff into useful leaf compost, a great garden soil amendment.

Grass clippings should be left in place as a natural source of nitrogen that returns to the soil during decomposition. Doing so helps gardeners reduce their chemical fertilizer habit while putting a dent in the shocking amount of grass and leaves Americans send to the dump each year, estimated to be 20 percent of the total waste stream (much higher in the peak growing months, lower in the off-season).

Each bag of clippings that was once carried away is equal to about one-quarter pound of usable nitrogen. Why throw out your back bagging clippings when they are a free, nontoxic source of lawn food? Even a light covering of leaves can simply be left in place and shredded on the spot during the final mowings of the season, although dried brown leaves are not rich in nitrogen (present in green plant material). They do, however, break down to return vital organic matter that builds soil.

The most dedicated ecology-minded gardeners will want to process everything on-site, even if their locality has a yard-waste recycling operation or they employ a lawn service that usually carts organic debris away. Why waste the fuel, hours of labor and dump fees or create pollution in the form of exhaust emissions required to truck the stuff away at all? Not to mention all those nasty, heavyweight plastic leaf bags that are used up in the process. Simply leave grass clippings right where they lie,

and shred, chip or compost everything else. Humus-rich compost can be put back into the garden soil in place of peat moss and other expensive, humus-rich soil amendments; chips can be used instead of bagged mulch.

Contrary to claims that leaving clippings on the lawn causes thatch buildup, they have nothing but good effects on turf grass that is mowed regularly. Grass blades are more than 70 percent water, soft tissue that when cut and left on the lawn quickly breaks down into useful, organic compounds. Thatch is mostly hard-to-break-down dead and dying stems.

For optimum lawn health, plan your mowing schedule so you remove about a third of the grass with each cutting. Any more, and the clippings will mat on the lawn surface, which is detrimental to general lawn health. If you have missed a mowing or two and create such long clippings, they should be raked up and composted in a bin instead.

Recycling mowers—also called self-mulching mowers—are another relatively new development equipped to handle not just grass clippings but even leaves. A mulching mower closely resembles a traditional mower, but instead of an ejector chute at one side of the deck, mulching mowers' decks are closed so that cut grass stays inside and gets thoroughly chopped up before falling onto the surface of the lawn. In the case of leaves, a second pass of the mower may be necessary to achieve small crumbs suitable for fast decomposition on the ground, or try pushing the mower more slowly.

Propagating Woody Groundcovers

Some groundcovering shrubs and vines can be propagated from soft-wood cuttings in summer, taken when the growth is neither too soft nor too hard to root well. Clematis, barberry, cotoneaster, deutzia, honeysuckle, Boston ivy, pyracantha, wisteria, trumpet vine and roses are good candidates. Here is the step-by-step procedure:

1. Fill a small, clean pot with a fast-draining but moisture-retentive soilless potting mix to which milled sphagnum, perlite, untreated kitty litter and coarse sand have been added.

2. In the morning, when plants contain maximum moisture, cut just above a leaf node, so you do not leave any stub of stem on the parent plant. Although with most plants you will only need cuttings with a few pairs of leaves, take long ones and trim them later. Make extras to allow for losses.

3. Trim each cutting by removing the top-most

pair of leaves (these are too soft and will wilt anyway) and trimming the stem just below the lowest pair of leaves you want to save. In a plant with long internodes (the length of stem between leaves), three pairs is fine. In others whose leaf nodes are tightly spaced, you may need 10 for a workable cutting. Remove any fruit or flowers and large bottom leaves.

4. Dip the bottom into clear water, then into rooting powder to hasten rooting and prevent rot and disease. Put a small amount of the powder into a saucer and dip the cutting into this; discard any of the unused, contaminated powder.

5. Poke a hole in the dampened potting medium so that it will be easy to stick the cutting in without knocking off all the powdered hormone. Place the cutting in the hole up to the second node, burying the lowest one. Firm medium gently.
6. Label the cuttings carefully, with name and date taken.

To make a softwood cutting, cut just above a leaf node, making sure the cutting will have about three pairs of leaves. Remove and discard the topmost pair of leaves. Dip the bottom end of the cutting into water, then in rooting hormone powder. Make a hole in a dampened growing medium with a pencil, then insert the cutting into the hole, being careful not to rub off the hormone powder.

7. Place the flats or pots inside a propagation sweatbox, easily made by bending wire coat hangers for a frame and covering with some dry-cleaning bags. A foil roasting pan is a perfect base. Place the home-made propagator in bright indirect light. At first, don't open—you'll lower the humidity. Then, after about two weeks, check for fallen leaves or rotted cuttings and remove them. Mist or water if needed.
Most plants will take four to eight weeks to

root well; once they are rooting, feed with a very dilute strength of fish emulsion or other natural liquid fertilizer. When they are well rooted, gradually open up the tent (one side every few days), then pot cuttings in roomier quarters, such as 3-inch pots. In late fall, they will require protection such as a cold frame; or try plunging the potted cuttings (bury potted plants to their rims) and mulching in a protected spot. The following spring, move into permanent positions.

Making Compost: Brown Plus Green Equals Black Gold

Don't be put off by intricate instructions on the labels of packaged compost starters or by the high prices of fancy tumblers, bins and cages deemed "essential" for making finished compost. Nature has been doing it quietly for an eternity without any of that stuff, and so can you. The bottom line of good compost: brown plus green equals black gold. I like to think of compost making as building a fire. You need various forms of fuel to make a good one, some that get going right away, some that are slower to ignite but burn longer.

To get compost cooking, a blend of materials that are nitrogen-rich (green, such as grass clippings) and ones that are carbon-rich (brown, such as dried leaves or wood shavings) makes the best recipe for success. The green is like kindling; the brown, particularly in the case of woody plant parts and slow-to-rot leaves (oak, for example) is like the larger logs. All that you'll need besides some of each is a shovelful of soil or finished compost every few layers (it's packed with the microorganisms that do the work of decomposing) and some moisture; these are the equivalent of the starter fluid and match.

A dry pile won't rot quickly; a soggy one won't, either, because oxygen will be missing, just as when you pile your logs too tightly in the fireplace and smother the flames. Air, fuel and moisture are the key elements. Turning the pile every now and then helps aerate it, although I must admit I have made many dozens of cubic yards of finished compost and have rarely turned a pile more than just occasionally. If you are willing to wait a year or more for it, and supply all the other elements, you can, too. Pile the debris so that the top of the heap (which should not be taller than about 5 feet) is concave, so rainwater can collect and seep into the middle.

A few other compost do's and dont's: Never put grease, fat or other animal products in the pile. Grease and fat will con-tribute to the smothering effect already mentioned; other animal foods are slow to decompose and will probably attract undesirables—rats, raccoons, opossums and the like.

Say no to used pet litter, because it may contain parasites. And don't put large or thick items in, even if they are vegetable in nature. They are just too slow and will muck up the works. Shred or chop citrus peels, for instance, to hasten decomposition, and do likewise with large pieces of spent plants from the garden, twigs, etc.

Coffee grounds, tea leaves, vegetable scraps, leftover pasta and rice— all are great for the heap. Dig them in a bit if animals are a worry. I put lightweight paper products like paper towels and coffee filters in the heap, tearing them up first. Newspaper will decompose, too, if used sparingly (it is considered "brown," by the way, as it's from wood), but because it is widely recycled, best to bundle it for pickup.

This compost starter bin is easy to make from four 4-foot posts, set in a rectangle, wrapped in chicken wire. If the chicken wire is secured loosely on the fourth side, the bin can be opened easily for removal of compost or for working the compost pile.

Can This Lawn Be Saved?

A stressful summer can bring out the worst in a lawn. If scorching weather has left its mark, late summer and fall is the time for renovation or replacement, because cooling trends and generally moister weather encourage good germination. New grass planted then will have most of a year to root before facing the test of summer heat. Is your lawn patchable, or does it need rejuvenation or total replacement? The basic rule of thumb: If 50 percent of it can be saved, if it is basically free of major weeds and if the thatch does not exceed 1.5 inches, you can get away with renovation.

Sometimes, all that's wrong is how you're caring for the lawn. It might need nothing more than aeration, dethatching, feeding, liming or a different watering routine. Selective pruning of overhanging trees can let more light in, which will give grass a boost. Take a turf sample into a cooperative extension office to test for bugs and diseases and a soil sample to test the pH.

Spot patching of areas damaged by construction, storms, heavy foot traffic or pets can really improve the look of certain lawns. Remove damaged turf, then rake and add topsoil as needed to achieve a proper grade; distribute seed, rake lightly, tamp down well and water thoroughly. A loose mulch of straw or peat moss can be used.

If patching isn't enough, partial renovation—overseeding the existing lawn—may be the solution, provided the grass is at least 50 percent salvageable, the thatch isn't too thick and the soil still drains well. First, the existing grass must be dealt with. Mow it very closely, then remove thatch with a heavy metal rake to expose a lot of soil. Rake up thatch and clippings. Dig out major weeds. Spread seed, rake gently, then cover raked seed with a sprinkling of soil, tamp down or roll, and water well.

In the worst of cases, when the ground is compacted and no longer drains well, the existing turf must be completely eliminated by mowing very short, then tilling under before amending the soil with several inches of organic matter such as peat and composted manure. Seed, roll and water; use a loose mulch layer if desired.

Annual bedding plants such as impatiens can be used to break up an otherwise all-lawn approach to landscaping.

PLANT PORTRAITS

More than 70 genera of recommended herbaceous (page 44) and woody (page 71) groundcovers are discussed in detail in this chapter, listed in alphabetical order according to the botanical, or Latin, name. In addition, a number of entries combining similar plants of more than one genus—Ferns, Moss and Mosslike Plants, Strawberry Look-Alikes, Succulents, Vines and Ornamental Grasses—are grouped under those English category titles. In all, then, here are portraits of more than 100 plants, with exceptional named varieties—those with showier leaves, bigger flowers or better overall performance, for instance—noted in many cases.

The Latin binomial (two-name) system of classifying plants may seem like a bother, but it actually makes things easier, helping to avert misunderstandings fostered by imprecise common names that may vary drastically from region to region. Take a stab at pronouncing the Latin names (a phonetic guide is given with each entry); even if you don't have a perfect accent, you will be much better understood than if you use the common name. The first name in the binomial is the genus, a grouping of plants with similar characteristics, such as *Ajuga* and *Cotoneaster*; the second name identifies the species, a smaller unit of classification indicating plants that are not only alike but can breed with each other. (Sometimes a third name follows, which may or may not be in Latin, denoting the subspecies, cultivar or variety, still more precise distinctions.)

Remember that almost any plant can be considered a groundcover.

PLANT PORTRAIT KEY

Here is a guide to the symbols and terms used throughout this section.

Latin name of the plant is in boldface italic.

Phonetic pronunciation of the Latin name is in parentheses.

Common name of the plant is in boldface type.

The average hours of sun needed per day is indicated by symbols. The first symbol is what the plant prefers, but the plant is adaptable to all conditions listed.

○ Sun—6 hours or more of strong, direct sunlight per day.
◑ Part shade—3 to 6 hours of direct sunlight per day.
● Shade—2 hours or less of direct sunlight per day.
💧 Drought resistant
⚱ Tolerant of wet soil
✳ Heat lover
❀ Long bloomer

Grade of Difficulty—Groundcovers that take the least amount of care are identified as *easy*. These plants are a good choice for beginning gardeners with little time.

Heights are for normal growth.

Zones—Check "The USDA Plant Hardiness Map of the United States" (page 92), based on average annual temperatures for each area—or zone—of the United States, to see which zone you live in. Every plant portrait lists the zones best for that plant.

Carol Mercer of the Secret Garden in East Hampton, Long Island, invokes a Japanese feeling by covering the ground beneath large boulders with velvety moss.

Cultural Information— Plants' preferences and information how best to grow your plants are given here. We recommend the easiest and best methods of increasing the number of your plants.

Those selected for inclusion here are 2 feet tall and under (with the exception of some of the ornamental grasses and the vines when grown upright) and were chosen for their popularity, ease of maintenance and availability. Although most gardeners would and do happily baby a few fussy plants for their startlingly beautiful flowers or some other irresistible quality, when planting large areas of groundcover, the last thing you want is finicky.

A final factor: If a plant that interests you really is considered more a flowering shrub, a perennial, an annual or an herb, it may not be covered in detail here. Referring to the other books in the Burpee American Gardening Series will expand your groundcover repertory manyfold.

HERBACEOUS GROUNDCOVERS

Aegopodium podagraria 'Variegatum' (ee-go-PO-dium) **goutweed, bishop's-weed, ground elder,** Easy, deciduous ○ ◑ ●
Zones: 3 to 9
Height: 6 to 12 inches
Flower Color: White
Characteristics: This herbaceous perennial can brighten even the dreariest spot in a flash, thanks to its highly variegated leaves of pale green edged liberally in white, and its energetic manner of spreading by underground rhizomes. The solid green form is simply too invasive, really more of a pesky weed. In late spring, umbels of white flowers like Queen Anne's lace appear, held in a stately manner above the foliage. Keep ahead of goutweed with regular root pruning (simply dig out any that has moved near or past its allotted boundary) and it will prove a rewarding, showy friend. Let it move into a perennial border, where it will quickly intertwine with every other root in its path, and you will be pulling out bits and pieces forever. Can be a dramatic edging plant along walkways, perhaps behind another zealous variegate, the dark green-and-silver *Lamiastrum Galeobdolon.*
Cultural Information: Goutweed likes good drainage, but don't treat it to top-quality garden soil or it will run even faster. Easy to propagate by digging out bits of rhizomes and simply relocating them. A great plant for sharing as there are always "spares."

Agave; see *Succulents*

Ajuga (aj-OOH-guh) **bugleweed,** Easy, semievergreen or evergreen ○ ◑ ●
Zones: 3 to 8
Height: 3 to 6 inches
Flower Colors: Blue, purple, red, white

Aegopodium *species*

Characteristics: A garden without *Ajuga* would be lacking indeed; this versatile, mat-forming carpeter features some of the showiest leaf markings of any perennial. Bugleweed is also an undemanding plant, eager to please. It increases in a healthy, but not impossibly invasive, manner by above-ground stolons (stems that root). Some of the flashiest named varieties for ground covering are *Ajuga reptans* 'Multicoloris' or *A. r.* 'Rainbow' (shiny green-bronze leaves with cream, red and yellow splotches, purple flowers); *A. r.* 'Variegata' (gray-green leaves mottled with cream, blue flowers); *A. r.* 'Bronze Beauty' or 'Atropurpurea' (purplish bronze leaves, purple flowers); and *A. r.* 'Burgundy Glow' (burgundy, pink, cream and green leaves, blue flowers). A mixed planting of adjacent waves of several varieties can be handsome, but over the long term, bugleweeds that are allowed to flower and set seed will begin to produce seedlings that may not be true to parental form. Rogue out any young uglies to preserve the design (and the gene pool). The clump-forming *A. pyramidalis* is better behaved and some gardeners prefer it for use in borders to *A. reptans*, but its foliage forms are not as showy. *A. p.* 'Metallica Crispa' is coppery, turning purple, with neat mounds of shiny leaves. *Ajuga* combines well at the front of the perennial border or along a path in part shade or moist sun with *Brunnera macrophylla* and *Alchemilla mollis*.

Cultural Information: Ajuga is a versatile grower, but prefers a soil with adequate moisture, where it will really thrive. Where *Ajuga* is planted up against a lawn, it likes to jump right into the grass, so it's best to leave a mowing strip or other barrier between the two; or let it go ahead and comingle, and enjoy the look—but don't expect to weed it out easily once this occurs. Divide in spring to increase stock.

Alchemilla (al-kem-ILL-uh) lady's-mantle, Moderate, deciduous ◗ 🪣

Zones: 3 to 8
Height: 6 to 12 inches
Flower Colors: Lime to chartreuse
Characteristics: The most familiar of the lady's-mantles, *A. mollis* (listed elsewhere in some sources as *A. vulgaris*) is one of those classics of English garden fame; gemlike dew droplets bead up on its velvety gray-green leaves, and above the vast mounds of foliage, frothy chartreuse flower sprays spill out from 200-foot-long borders onto centuries-old stone paths. In the favorably moist English climate, approximated only in our Pacific Northwest if anywhere in the United States, such things are possible, and *A. mollis* is even a prodigious self-sower. But in most American gardens, the picture will be a bit (or a lot) more restrained. *Alchemilla* won't grow into great drifts in the South, for instance. *A. mollis* is great for obscuring ripening foliage of minor spring bulbs when its fresh leaves emerge from a winter's nap. *A. alpina* is smaller-leaved and shorter (about 6 inches); its deeply cut foliage is edged in a narrow band of silvery white. It is less commonly grown and slightly

Ajuga reptans *'Silver Beauty'*

Ajuga reptans

Alchemilla alpina

Alchemilla mollis

less heat-tolerant, although quite charming.

Cultural Information: Soil moisture—anything short of boggy conditions—is what this plant requires. Do not expect much in hot, dry environs. *Alchemilla* needs at least part sun to flower well but cannot withstand full sun unless its moisture requirements are well met. *Alchemillas* may be slow to settle in, but give them time. Freshen up in

Anaphalis margaritacea

Antennaria *with* Ajuga

midsummer or any other time the leaves look tired by pinching off any older, damaged foliage; you will be rewarded with a fresh crop. Or, cut down the plants after flowering for a complete new flush of growth if weather conditions have sapped it or it has been otherwise damaged. Increase by seed, division.

Aloe; see *Succulents*

Alumroot; see *Heuchera*

American barrenwort; see *Vancouveria*

Anaphalis (an-NAFF-al-iss) **everlasting,** Easy, deciduous, native ○◗
Zones: 3 to 9
Height: 2 to 3 feet
Flower Color: White
Characteristics: A. margaritacea, pearly everlasting, is an erect native perennial grown not just for its buttonlike white flowers in late summer (great dried for winter arrangements) but also for its silvery, felted foliage. It is an important food source for caterpillars of various painted-lady species of butterflies, including the American painted lady. Many nurseries sell a non-native form, the one of Indian origin properly called *A. cinnamomea,* instead of the American, which it strongly resembles.
Cultural Information: Anaphalis is a sun lover that can withstand drought, but the foliage will be at its best with good soil moisture, unlike many other gray-leaved plants that resent even a hint of moist feet. Can become invasive; divide every three to four years. Increase by division.

Antennaria dioica (an-ten-AR-eee-uh die-oh-EE-kah) **pussy-toes,** Easy, semievergreen ○
Zones: 3 to 8
Height: 4 to 12 inches
Flower Colors: White, rose
Characteristics: Foliage is the principal asset of this mat-forming, stoloniferous perennial; it changes from fuzzy gray early in the season to gray-green and even green by season's end. It is a rock-garden subject that can be tucked successfully into the cracks in a walkway or patio or massed in other hot, dry sites. Preferred food of the larval stage (caterpillar) of the American painted lady butterfly. The cultivar *A. d.* 'Minima' makes a thick inch-tall carpet. *A. d.* 'Rosea' has pink blooms, and is about 4 inches tall.
Cultural Information: Will tolerate dry, infertile soils and heat. Good drainage preferred; sandy soil fine. Divide in spring to increase.

Arabis (AR-ah-bis) **rock cress, wall cress,** Easy, evergreen ○
Zones: 4 to 9
Height: 6 to 12 inches
Flower Colors: White, rose, pink
Characteristics: The various forms of *Arabis,* as the common names suggest, are well suited to use in the rockery, meaning that they are accustomed to lean, dry, hot conditions. They make good edgers or fillers for cracks in pavement and are quite ornamental. *A. caucasia* 'Variegata' has showy yellow stripes on the soft whitish green leaves. There is also a variegated-leaf form of *A. procurrens,* the leaves of which are shiny green. *A. procurrens* can tolerate light shade.

currens can tolerate light shade. Use these variegates at the front of a design as a focal point. *Cultural Information:* Most of the *Arabis* like limy, well-drained soil that is lean. To keep plantings looking dense and tidy, shear after flowering is finished (cut back by about half). Increase by division.

Archangel, yellow; see *Lamiastrum*

Asarum (as-AR-um) **wild ginger,** Moderate, evergreen or deciduous, many natives ◐ ●
Zones: Various
Height: 6 to 12 inches
Flower Color: Greenish or purplish brown, insignificant
Characteristics: This genus of woodland residents, most of them highly ornamental, are grown for their foliage. Curiously shaped flowers are borne near ground level and are usually obscured by the leaves, thereby rendered insignificant from the gardener's point of view. Although their root stocks smell spicy and gingerlike, they are not related to the culinary herb (*Zingiber officinale*, an East Indies native).

Among the American wild ginger natives, *A. hartwegii*, the cyclamen-leaved ginger (4 to 6 inches, Zones 5 to 9), is the showiest. It has evergreen, kidney-shaped leaves marbled in silver. Another native, *A. canadense* (deciduous, 6 to 8 inches, Zones 2 to 9), has dark green, heart-shaped leaves up to 6 inches across; because it dies back to the ground, it is best for less prominent locations, but it is the hardiest of the clan. The southern wild ginger, *A. shuttle-*

worthii, is also a native plant (5 to 8 inches; Zones 7 to 9, 6 with protection). It is evergreen except in the coldest parts of its range, and the foliage is glossy and marked in silver. An increasingly popular import, *A. europaeum*, the European wild ginger (6 inches, Zones 4 to 8), is elegant and evergreen to boot with 2- to 3-inch, polished green leaves. The gingers' heart-shaped leaves are a good complement to those of *Astilbe*, ferns, *Iris cristata* and lilyturf (*Liriope*). Remember the name *Asarum* in-

Arabis albida 'Flore-plena'

Asarum canadense

stead of *Vinca* or *Pachysandra* the next time you want an evergreen groundcover.

Cultural Information: The wild gingers are residents of the woodland floor, so they appreciate moist, well-drained, humus-rich soil and a shady exposure (dappled light or shade). Slugs and snails can be troublesome. Increase by division.

Astilbe 'Sprite'

Astilbe ×Arendsii *hybrids*

Asperula odorata; see *Galium odoratum*

Astilbe (as-TILL-be) **astilbe,** Easy, deciduous ◑ ○
Zones: 4 to 8
Height: 8 to 24 inches
Flower Colors: Pink, white, cream, red, peach, lilac
Characteristics: Astilbes are certainly among the best groundcovers for moist shade, the condition most of them consider ideal. Besides offering handsome, ferny foliage (in varied, striking shades of green through coppery red), they have plumelike long-lasting inflorescences that hold up well dried, either right in place in the garden where they will catch the snow or cut for indoor arrangements. The more soil moisture, the more sun astilbes can take. One of the best lower-growing subjects from this vast, much-hybridized genus includes *Astilbe chinensis pumila*, which grows to about 1 foot, is a fine front-of-the-border plant and is striking along walkways; this fast-spreading mat former with long-lasting red-pink flowers (pale mauve in the named selection *A. c.* 'Finale') in summer can withstand drier soils than many astilbes. The class of *A.* ×*Arendsii* hybrids, many about 2 feet high, includes such stars as *A. A.* 'Fanal' (bronze foliage and red plumes). The *A.* ×*Arendsii* hybrids are what gardeners will recognize as the classic astilbe; the vast majority of astilbes sold are in this group. *A. simplicifolia* 'Sprite', just under 1 foot high with shell pink flowers, is another fine groundcover, although somewhat slower to establish.

Punctuate a mass of white-flowered astilbes with a grouping of large, white-margined hostas. For longest season of bloom, as long as mid-June into September, incorporate several astilbes in a design. Astilbes work well with ferns, too, whose foliage is also lacy but a contrasting, more yellow green, and less opaque.

Cultural Information: Deep, organically rich soils with adequate moisture and part shade preferred, but astilbes can be grown in full sun in moderate zones provided they are not exposed to drought. These heavy feeders appreciate a topdressing of several inches of composted manure every spring, and division every three or four years.

Barren strawberry; see *Strawberry Look-Alikes*

Barrenwort; see *Epimedium*

Barrenwort, American; see *Vancouveria*

Bells, oconee; see *Shortia*

Bergenia (ber-GEN-ee-uh) **bergenia,** Moderate, semievergreen ◑
Zones: 3 or 4 to 9
Height: 1 to 2 feet
Flower Colors: Pink, white, salmon, purple, red
Characteristics: Gertrude Jekyll, the legendary English garden designer, knew a good garden plant, and this was one of her favorites. Shiny, thick leaves take on a purplish-bronze cast in cold weather and grow in large clumps that resemble loose cabbage heads. Those of *B. cordifolia*, the heartleaf bergenia, are about 10 inches long; in *B.*

crassifolia, the leather bergenia, they can be up to 18 inches long and more oval in shape. The 'Bressingham' hybrids are particularly handsome. Attractive flowers are produced by all bergenias in spring, emerging up on stalks from the center of the foliage mounds, although they may be nipped by harsh winters. No matter, really, because bergenia is such a fine foliage plant, excellent in swaths along pathways, at the front of flower beds and wrapping around corners of borders for a classic English feel. Combine with contrasting foliage of yucca or feathery gray artemisia for maximum impact.

Cultural Information: Bergenias can tolerate more sun (and in fact its foliage will be most colorful in good light) in northern climates than in the South. Tolerant of various soils, but will grow lushly when it is humus rich. Bergenia's semievergreen foliage will need some preening to remove winter-damaged leaves. Divide in spring after flowering to increase stock. Keep ahead of slugs.

Bishop's hat; see ***Epimedium***

Bishop's-weed; see ***Aegopodium***

Bloodroot; see ***Sanguinaria***

Brunnera macrophylla
(BRUN-er-a mak-ro-FILL-a) **heart-leaf brunnera, Siberian bugloss,** Easy, deciduous ◑ ○
Zones: 4 to 8
Height: 12 to 18 inches

Flower Color: Blue
Characteristics: Brunnera's dark green, heart-shaped leaves get bigger as the season progresses, forming sumptuous mounds that are topped in early spring with blue flowers reminiscent of forget-me-nots. The foliage is rough-textured, as anyone who has handled the plant will surely attest. Brunnera's foliage forms a fine contrast to astilbes and ferns, and also to lady's-mantles. A variegated selection called *B. m.* 'Dawson's White', or 'Variegata', is harder to find, but very showy, and requires a bit more protection than the plain green. Naturalized in large sweeps under deciduous trees, Brunnera is outstanding.

Cultural Information: Pay attention to available soil moisture, particularly when brunnera is grown in sun. As is the case with other large-leaved plants, slugs and snails like it. Divide after flowering to propagate.

Bugleweed; see ***Ajuga***

Bugloss, Siberian; see ***Brunnera***

Cerastium (ser-ASS-tee-um) **snow-in-summer,** Easy, evergreen ○ ◖
Zones: 2 to 8
Height: 4 to 6 inches
Flower Color: White
Characteristics: Cerastium is cultivated for its fast-growing low mat of silvery foliage, topped (in summer, of course) by a virtual blizzard of white flowers. *C. tomentosum*, the most familiar garden form, is a good edger along walkways in sunny hot spots and is fine for use in pavement nooks and crannies, too.

Bergenia *'Bressingham White'*

Brunnera macrophylla

Cerastium tomentosum

Ceratostigma plumbaginoides

Chrysanthemum pacificum

Cultural Information: These favorite rockery plants will grow even in sand, so be certain to ensure fast drainage. In the South, partial shade can be tolerated. *Cerastium* appreciates a bit of pruning in early spring, to tidy up the foliage. Grow from seed sown in spring or late summer for bloom the next year, from divisions or from cuttings of fresh growth in mid- to late summer.

Ceratostigma plumbaginoides (cer-at-OS-tig-ma plumbah-gi-NOI-deez) **leadwort,** Easy, deciduous to semievergreen ○ ◑

Zones: 5 to 9
Height: 8 to 12 inches
Flower Color: Blue
Characteristics: Slow-to-awaken, wiry-stemmed leadwort more than makes up for its initial hesitation with blue flowers from late summer into fall and stunning bronze-red fall foliage. It is a great companion for small spring bulbs, concealing their messy ripening leaves as the season progresses, later putting on a display of its own.

Cultural Information: Leadwort is tolerant of a variety of soils, light and moisture conditions. Apply a winter mulch for added protection in coolest part of range; in areas where growing season is long, leadwort's flowers, slow to be formed, can be appreciated most. In zones where the leaves persist over the winter, cut them back in early spring to encourage fresh growth. Increase by spring division.

Chameleon plant; see *Houttuynia*

Christmas rose; see *Helleborus*

Chrysanthemum pacificum (kris-ANTH-em-um pa-CIF-ickum) **gold-and-silver chrysanthemum,** Easy, deciduous ○ ◑

Zones: 5 to 9
Height: 1 foot
Flower Color: Yellow
Characteristics: A relative newcomer to the American nursery industry, this native Japanese species has dense rosettes of striking green foliage edged in a slender band of silvery white. Almost as quickly as it became available, it was renamed *Ajania pacifica*, in the great shake-up of the *Chrysanthemum* genus that left few survivors. Even if you live too far north to benefit from more than a short display of the late-season gold button flowers, *C. pacificum* is a great addition to the groundcover repertory.

Chrysogonum virginianum

Cultural Information: C. pacificum prefers a sunny site and sharp drainage for peak performance, but will grow in part shade. It can tolerate sandy soils of the seashore garden and is handsome as an undulating groundcover on slopes. May be grown north to Zone 4 with protection. Divide in spring to increase.

Chrysogonum virginianum (kris-OG-oh-num vir-gin-ee AY-num) **golden star, green and gold,** Easy, semievergreen to deciduous, native ◐ ●

Zones: 5 to 9
Height: 6 to 8 inches
Flower Color: Yellow
Characteristics: Golden star is an extremely popular garden plant because it produces a long display of showy, daisylike flowers in part shade or shade, not a common trait. It is low growing with hairy leaves, and most at home and most appropriate aesthetically in the naturalistic setting of the woodland garden. *C. v.* 'Mark Viette' is a dwarf cultivar; *C. v.* 'Allen Bush' blooms all spring long.
Cultural Information: Grow *Chrysogonum* in the moisture-retentive, organic soil common to the woodland floor. It can tolerate part sun in the cooler zones of its range if adequate soil moisture is available. Increase by division.

Comfrey; see *Symphytum*

Convallaria majalis (kon-val-AIR-ee-uh mah-JAL-iss) **lily of the valley,** Easy, deciduous, Native ◐ ●

Zones: 2 to 8
Height: 8 inches
Flower Colors: White, pink
Characteristics: Who does not know the fragrance of lily of the valley, or its diminutive stems of white nodding bells? Lily of the valley is a sturdy and enthusiastic groundcover, particularly for humus-rich, moist, shady sites such as the woodland garden or below shrubs and trees elsewhere in the landscape. However, the foliage will tend to look beat up by late summer and will disappear gradually, leaving a blank spot in the garden picture, so plan accordingly. Some bulbs of the autumn-flowering crocus (*Colchicum*) could brighten the "empty" spot in fall or simply clean up *Convallaria*'s spent foliage and replenish the mulch over its bed for a tidy fall-into-winter appearance.
Cultural Information: *Convallaria majalis* likes an adequate supply of soil moisture; in dry exposures, it will be less zealous. In the heat of the South, lily of the valley may not flower reliably. Overcrowded beds in need of division will also fail to flower well. To care for established plantings, top-dress with 1 or 2 inches of rotted manure when dormant in the fall. Divide the pips, as the individual rooted divisions are called, after flowering or in fall.

Coralbells; see *Heuchera*

Cranesbill; see *Geranium*

Creeping jennie; see *Lysimachia*

Cress, rock; see *Arabis*

Cress, wall; see *Arabis*

Convallaria majalis

Cyclamen (CYKE-la-men) **hardy cyclamen,** Moderate, deciduous to semievergreen ◐ ●

Zones: 5 to 9 or 7 to 9, by species
Height: 4 to 6 inches
Flower Colors: Pinks, white, red
Characteristics: The florist's cyclamen, *C. persicum*, is a well-known Easter and Mother's Day gift, with flashily colored flowers and intricately marbled foliage, each plant's leaves appearing unique in its markings. But there are hardy cyclamen for

Cyclamen *species*

the garden, too, and although lesser known, they are sure to enjoy increasing popularity as word of their special charm filters out. Who could fail to be captivated by blossoms like pastel butterflies with swept-back wings? Long appreciated in British gardens, and among certain savvy sorts in the American Southeast, they are colonizers grown from corms (a kind of thickened underground stem resembling a bulb) that in time mature and reproduce to make a breathtaking low groundcover for the connoisseur's garden. Cyclamen go dormant part of the year, meaning that their leaves disappear sometime after flowering is complete. They are wonderful from fall into winter, but their rest period later on will leave gaps—a small price to pay for such a performance at a time when not much else is happening in many gardens. In the woodland, nature's own ever-replenishing groundcover of leaf litter looks just fine; in the naturalistic garden, it is a more appropriate choice than overplanting the cyclamen with flashy bedding annuals.

The two species most adaptable to the garden are _C. coum_ (hardy to Zone 7, blooms about December to March, rounded, heart-shaped leaves) and the easiest of all to cultivate, _C. hederifolium_ (to Zone 5, formerly _C. neapolitanum_, blooms in fall, flowers may precede emergence of pointed, ivylike leaves). Grow them under trees and shrubs or alongside pathways where visitors can stoop and have a closer look at these charmers.

Because some purveyors collect them from the wild in their Mediterranean homelands to sell to customers, a practice that threatens the survival of the plants in their original habitat, it is important to determine the source of the cyclamen you are buying. Be sure it is a nursery grown one, not collected from the wild.

Cultural Information: Particularly useful in the woodland for naturalizing, where ants will gladly carry the minuscule seeds about to start new plantings, and also in the dry shade of oaks and evergreens. Most cyclamen like alkaline soil that is humus rich. Planting is easiest during summer dormancy, when the corms can be placed ½ inch or so below the soil surface. Except when getting new plantings set in place, do not water while dormant; at other times in the season, be certain that cyclamen are not subjected to soggy soil.

Daylily; see _**Hemerocallis**_

Dead nettle; see _**Lamium**_

Duchesnea; see _**Strawberry Look-Alikes**_

Echeveria; see _**Succulents**_

**Epimedium** (ep-i-MEE-dium) **bishop's hat, barrenwort,** Easy, most evergreen or semievergreen ● ◑
Zones: 3 or 4 to 8 or 9
Height: 6 to 12 inches
Flower Colors: Yellow, white, rose, lilac, bicolors
Characteristics: Like the tortoise, the barrenworts are slow but they are winners. Give them time to establish and they will create attractive masses of groundcover, even in the dense shade of large trees where there is much root competition. The leaves are held aloft on wiry stems; the flowers, which are like so many tiny dancing columbines on wires of their own, are charming, borne in spring. In some species, the foliage takes on reddish or bronze casts or margins early in the season; others, including _E. grandiflorum_ (Zones 3 to 8), color up this way in late summer or fall. _E. g._ 'Rose Queen' and _E. g._ 'White Queen' are recommended.
Cultural Information: Because these are very long-lived plants, add lots of organic matter such as peat moss to the soil before planting. _Epimedium_ can withstand occasional haircuts if the foliage looks ratty. Divide in spring or fall to increase.

Everlasting, pearly; see _**Anaphalis**_

**Ferns,** various species, Easy, evergreen to deciduous, many natives ● ◑ ♟
Zones: Various, by species
Height: Several inches to tree height
Characteristics: "God made ferns

Epimedium _species_

to show what He could do with leaves," wrote Henry David Thoreau. Ferns have a magical grace that cannot be matched by any other garden plant. Perhaps it is the fact that they are among the planet's oldest flora, dating back in their evolution some 300 to 400 million years, long before the flowering plants many of us fill our gardens with exclusively. But even without the garnish of flowers, ferns have much to commend them. One need only watch the emergence of the season's fresh crop of crosiers (fiddleheads), the tightly furled fronds-to-be, to be completely captivated. Even dappled woodland light positively electrifies the transparent green foliage of many ferns, and then there is the arrangement of the dustlike spores into brown bumps or strips called *sori*—like papery strips of dot candy in some species and an entire coating of velvet in others.

Some favorites for groundcover include Christmas fern (*Polystichum acrostichoides*, Zones 3 to 9), a low, evergreen fern of moist woodlands, whose common name comes not from the fact that it is evergreen but because each of the leaflets on its fronds is notched to form a tiny Christmas stocking; Japanese painted fern (*Athyrium goeringianum* 'Pictum', Zones 3 to 8), with variegated gray-and-chocolate foliage (select carefully, because each plant's markings are distinct and highly variable; what you see is what you get); and the maidenhair fern (*Adiantum pedatum*, Zones 3 to 8), which with its black, wiry stems and extremely delicate, fresh green fronds seems

to dance in the breeze.

The New York (*Thelypteris noveboracensis*), hay-scented (*Dennstaedtia punctilobula*) and sensitive ferns (*Onoclea sensibilis*) will quickly spread into large masses, a plus or a minus depending on where you place them. Members of the genus *Woodwardia* (the chain ferns) do well in swampy sites; the sensitive fern will withstand marshy soils, as will the interrupted fern (*Osmunda claytoniana*) and ostrich fern (*Matteuccia Struthiopteris pensylvanica*), a relative giant of up to 5 feet high. In tropical climates such as Florida, sword fern (*Nephrolepis*) or leatherleaf fern (*Rumohra*), each 1 to 3 feet high, are good options for groundcover.

When designing with ferns, the best effect can be achieved by combining several species. Punctuate large drifts of two or three low-growing selections with such exclamation points as Goldie's fern (*Dryopteris goldiana*), golden when first opening and light green once fully unfurled, when it reaches about 4 feet in height. The Japanese painted fern makes another fine accent. With hostas and astilbes, ferns have become a shade-gardening tradition of easy care and lasting attractiveness.

Cultural Information: Most ferns cultivated in garden settings like moist, woodsy soil on the acid side and part shade, but there are many exceptions in the vast world of the *Pterydophyta*, the oldest category of plants that produce neither cones (as do the slightly newer *Gymnospermae*) nor flowers (like the "modern" *Angiospermae*). There are tiny aquatic ferns, and oth-

Athyrium goeringianum 'Pictum'

Osmunda cinnamomea

ers of tree proportions that prosper in tropical zones, and even desert species. In the woodland or shade garden, however, you will generally be dealing with shallow-rooted plants that appreciate loose soil and a light mulch of rotted leaves, what they would get in their native habitat. Divide to increase, most easily accomplished when they are dormant; reproduction by spores is too slow for the gardener with ground to cover.

Foamflower; see *Tiarella*

Fragaria; see *Strawberry Look-Alikes*

Funkia; see *Hosta*

Galax urceolata

Galium odoratum

Geranium macrorrhizum

Galax (GAY-lacks) **wandflower,** Easy, evergreen, native ●

Zones: 3 to 8

Height: 6 inches

Flower Color: White

Characteristics: Shiny, low rosettes of leathery leaves up to 4 inches across take on a bronze cast in winter, making this eastern American native a great groundcover for the shade of shrubs and deciduous trees. *Galax* sends up erect wands of white flowers in late spring. Sold variously as *G. urceolata* or *G. aphylla.*

Cultural Information: Dig in plenty of peat moss to create the highly organic, moisture-retentive, slightly acidic conditions *Galax* prefers. Divide in spring or fall to increase.

Galium odoratum (GAY-lee-um oh-door-RAH-tum) **sweet woodruff,** Easy, deciduous ● ●🜂

Zones: 4 to 9

Height: 6 inches

Flower Color: White

Characteristics: Sweet woodruff (sometimes listed as *Asperula odorata*) has several charms: Its pointed, linear leaves are arranged in whorls, like the petals of a daisy; they are fragrant, used in sachets and in May wine; when it blooms in spring, its tiny white flowers lend a delicate beauty to the garden floor. *Galium odoratum* makes a fine underplanting for rhododendron and other shrubs that share its taste for moist, somewhat acid soil. Lovely naturalized in large sweeps in the woodland garden. Some weedier relatives are American natives, but do not make good garden subjects. The cultivated variety already mentioned hails from Asia and Europe.

Cultural Information: A rapid grower with a taste for moisture. Propagate by division.

Geranium (ger-AY-knee-um) **hardy geranium, cranesbill,** Easy, deciduous or semi-evergreen ○ ●

Zones: 4 to 10

Height: 6 to 24 inches

Flower Colors: Pink, reddish, white, violet, salmon

Characteristics: These are not the so-called geraniums so commonly potted up each summer by gardeners; those are actually members of the genus *Pelargonium* and not *Geranium* at all. The hardy geraniums are generally low, somewhat sprawling perennials, with handsome leaves that are palmate and often deeply lobed like a Japanese maple's, and springtime flowers not unlike those of the *Pelargonium* clan. The bigroot geranium (*G. macrorrhizum,* 12 to 18 inches) has great fall color and is the one that really requires a shady exposure; its large, aromatic leaves are semi-evergreen. A shaded bank of it would be splendid through most seasons. Bloody cranesbill (*G. sanguineum,* 12 to 18 inches) tolerates even full sun; the variety *G. s. prostratum* is a compact form only 6 inches high. *G.* × 'Johnson's Blue' (18 to 24 inches tall) flowers over a long season with violet blooms. In hot locations, grow it in part shade.

Cultural Information: Geraniums like well-drained soil. Many will rebloom if deadheaded, or they can be shorn to the ground after the first show of flowers fades and fed and watered so they will grow again and rebloom later in the season (do not shear *G. macrorrhizum*, because its leaves are nearly evergreen). Divide, or grow from seed.

Ginger, wild; see *Asarum*

Gold-and-silver chrysanthemum; see *Chrysanthemum*

Goldenstar; see *Chrysogonum*

Goutweed; see *Aegopodium*

Grass, Mondo; see *Ophiopogon*

Green and gold; see *Chrysogonum*

Ground elder; see *Aegopodium*

Hardy cyclamen; see *Cyclamen*

Hardy geranium; see *Geranium*

Heartleaf; see *Brunnera*

Hellebore; see *Helleborus*

Helleborus (hell-e-BOR-us) **hellebore, Lenten** or **Christmas rose,** Moderate, evergreen to semievergreen ◑ ●
Zones: 3 to 9, depending on variety
Height: 12 to 24 inches
Flower Colors: Green, white, pink, purple, bicolors
Characteristics: Who would not

love a plant that sent up long-lasting, nodding flowers right through a crust of snow, whose leathery foliage persisted through almost every turn of weather imaginable in fine form? It is hard to imagine why more American gardeners have not dug out portions of their beds of pachysandra, *Vinca*, and ivy in favor of hellebores, which like moist, humus-rich woodsy soil but can even tolerate the drier shade beneath deciduous trees. Plant with other evergreen groundcovers such as Christmas fern and wild ginger for year-'round appeal or with a variegated creeping groundcover beneath it, such as *Lamiastrum*, *Lamium* or even a green-and-white form of *Vinca*.

Among the hellebores, the unfortunately named stinking hellebore (*H. foetidus*, Zones 6 to 9) has deeply divided leaves and sends up red-margined pale green blooms in late winter and early spring. Combine it with big-leaved hostas for good contrast. The Corsican hellebore (*H. lividus corsicus*, Zones 7 to 9), has paler green leaves than the rest and is marbled. Flowers, appearing in late winter, are yellow-green blushed with purple. The Christmas rose (*H. niger*, Zones 3 to 9) produces low mounds of dark green foliage and white flowers blushed with pink that may miss the holiday season. The Lenten rose (*H. orientalis*, Zones 6 to 9) offers white, pink or purple flowers in winter or early spring.
Cultural Information: Many gardeners make a habit of cutting off old, damaged leaves in earliest spring, as flower buds develop, to encourage fresh new

Helleborus orientalis

growth. Doing so may also improve flower show, because in many cases blossoms are obscured by foliage. Divide in autumn to increase stock, but do so with care, as they don't like to be moved. Also grown from seed; cross-pollination by hand has produced some dramatic flower colors and forms.

Hemerocallis (hem-er-oh-KAL-iss) **daylily,** Easy, deciduous ○ ◑
Zones: 3 to 10
Height: 18 inches to 5 feet
Flower Colors: All but pure white and true blue
Characteristics: Among the easiest of the garden perennials, daylilies double in number every year to boot, making them great groundcover candidates. Their arcing, straplike foliage is graceful and makes a great border between the edge of the lawn and the trees beyond, along foundations of buildings, beside walkways or against fences. Although bloom may be diminished by low-light conditions, many daylilies will produce great masses of foliage for groundcover even in the dappled light of a woodland setting. An island of

Hemerocallis 'Stella d'Oro'

daylilies is an easy-care way to break up all that lawn, and the fleshy roots thwart all but the most insistent weeds and hold the soil firmly in place in areas prone to erosion. Bloom is possible from June into September with careful planning; combine early-, mid- and late-season varieties into each design. For an even longer display, spring through fall, interplant with clumps of various daffodils (early-, mid- and late-season varieties); these virtually carefree bulbs have only one drawback: their slow-to-ripen, unsightly foliage, which the daylily leaves will graciously hide.

The latest hybrids are often tetraploids; that is, they have double the number of chromosomes per cell that a daylily is

Heuchera *species*

meant to, 44 instead of 22. Tetraploidy is accomplished by plant breeders with the application of a chemical that stops normal cell division. Visually, tetraploids are different from such "unimproved" originals as the famous roadside tawny daylily (*H. fulva*); the latest flowers tend to be very large and are held lower on thicker scapes (stems), but in the most extreme cases risk looking more like a hibiscus to my eye than a daylily. The new hybrids, some of them fetching three-figure prices per plant, do feature more flowers per scape (each lasts only a day, so that means longer bloom), a wide range of colors and other improvements, however. There are more than 30,000 named cultivars to select from. 'Stella d'Oro' is a miniature, long-blooming yellow that is only about 1 foot high, making a great edger or low cover. 'Franz Hals', just under 2 feet, is a smashing bicolor of rust and gold.

Cultural Information: Daylilies like an evenly moist soil; if they dry out too much, particularly in the period leading up to flowering, blooms will be diminished. Top-dress with rotted manure before foliage emerges in late winter to early spring. If foliage looks tattered in midsummer, cut it back and a fresh show will emerge. Divide anytime to increase.

Heuchera (hew-KER-uh) **alumroot, coralbells,** Easy, evergreen to semievergreen, native ◖ ○
Zones: 4 to 8
Height: 1 to 2 feet

Flower Colors: White, pink, red, coral
Characteristics: Mounds of evergreen or nearly evergreen foliage and tall, long-lasting sprays of delicate flowers give the *Heuchera* genus much to recommend it. The leaves of *Heuchera* are variously reminiscent of *Pelargonium* (what we commonly call geraniums), maples and ivies. Some varieties have hairy leaves. With the promotion of the relatively recent selection *H. micrantha* 'Palace Purple', the gardener also has a bronze-to-purple foliage form readily available; it is about 2 feet high. Choose carefully when buying 'Palace Purple' plants, as they appear to be highly variable in leaf color; the color also washes out somewhat as the summer progresses in sunny exposures. *H. americana* is a native of the dry woodlands, fine for shady, dry sites and a bit bigger than the rest—a good choice for the southern garden. *H. sanguinea*, the one known as coralbells, is likely to be closer to just a foot tall, with its flower stalks—the part that evokes the common name, although the bells come in white, too—considerably higher. It is happy in sun, except in the hottest zones. Fine along walkways and anywhere that a tidy, persistent show of attractive foliage is desired. Use 'Palace Purple' at the front of a planting of such groundcovers as yellow-leaved *Hosta* and the leathery dark green of *Bergenia* for color contrasts. It is also fine against the lacy silver foliage of *Artemisia schmidtiana* 'Silver Mound' and 'Powis Castle'.
Cultural Information: A reliable,

long-lived plant that will thank you for an organic soil, part shade and adequate soil moisture, but can tolerate a little less than perfection if so required. Divide to increase stock.

Hosta (HOS-ta) **plantain lily, funkia, hosta,** Easy, deciduous ◐ ●

Zones: 3 to 8 or 9
Height: 3 to 36 inches and higher
Flower Colors: White, lilac
Characteristics: It would be impossible to overrate hostas for their value in the shady garden. I think that they are beautiful from the very first unfurled tubes of foliage that poke through the ground in spring to their very last stand, yellowed, almost limp, and about to droop, come fall. In between, there is a feast of blue-green and gray-green and yellow-green, pure greens both dark and pale, and foliage that is pure gold or heavily marked with cream or cleaner white. Hostas don't skimp on leaf texture, either. If you like them curled or twisted, puckered or ribbed, take your pick. As for finish, it runs from frosted, matte surfaces like 'Krossa Regal', to a polished shine. Such dwarfs as *H. venusta* have their own charm, providing a fine groundcover when a diminutive scale is appropriate, but so do the relative giants of the *H. sieboldiana* lineage, including such stars as *H. s.* 'Frances Williams' (blue-green edged in gold) and *H. s.* 'Elegans' (puckered blue leaves, mounding to 3 feet high and even bigger across). With all this potential, don't succumb to the dreary approach of mass after mass of one variety alone. Play hostas, with their substantial leaves, against the delicate foliage of ferns and astilbes. Interplanted with variegated Solomon's seal (*Polygonatum odoratum* 'Variegatum'), Japanese jack-in-the-pulpit (*Arisaema sikokianum*) or the purple-leaved snakeroot (*Cimicifuga ramosa* 'Atropurpurea'), they are brilliant, too. The golden-leaves hostas are particularly useful for lighting up otherwise all-green plantings. Try 'Zounds', nearly metallic and just under 2 feet high; 'Gold Standard', 24 inches with green margins; *H. plantaginea* 'Piedmont Gold', 18 inches with plentiful white flowers; and 'Shademaster', 24 inches, a good gold form for shadier areas (generally speaking, golden-leaved plants need part sun to color up best, although they may crisp in too much direct sun). For a tiny gold form, 'Lights Up' at about 3 inches high may be just the thing. Spring bulbs under hostas are a perfect pairing.
Cultural Information: These are really durable creatures—plantings thirty years old and older are not uncommon. If deprived of moisture, hosta leaves will start to get crisp from the edges inward. In certain cooler regions along the coast, it is possible to expose some hostas to sun. But for southern gardens and other sunny spots, *H. plantaginea* is perhaps the most receptive to light and heat of all. A bonus: It has some of the most beautiful, fragrant flowers of the genus, large, white and borne late summer. Hybrids of *H. plantaginea* include the named varieties 'Piedmont Gold', 'Royal Standard' and 'Honeybells'. Generally, blue-leaved hostas are most desirous of shade and moisture; gold-leaved ones are frequently somewhat sun tolerant. Divide to increase. Unfortunately, hosta leaves are a favorite food of slugs and snails.

Hosta *'Kabitan'*

Hosta Sieboldiana *'Elegans'*

Houttuynia cordata 'Chameleon'

Lamium maculatum

Lamiastrum galeobdolon

Houttuynia (hoo-TIE-nee-a) chameleon plant, Easy, deciduous ◐ ● ✿

Zones: 5 to 10
Height: 6 to 18 inches
Flower Color: White
Characteristics: Chameleon plant, an aggressive groundcover for shady locations, has heart-shaped foliage that emits an orangey fragrance when bruised. *H. cordata* 'Variegata', or 'Chameleon', is desirable for its heavily mottled leaves splashed with red, cream, pink, yellow and green—a real attention getter in the shaded garden. Treat it as you would any invasive plant by containing it in sunken pots, or digging out wandering rhizomes promptly—or give it a large space of its own, if its flashy colors appeal. Startling with variegated ribbon grass (*Phalaris arundinacea picta*) or the red-striped Japanese blood grass (*Imperata cylindrica* 'Rubra') plus a splash of yellow feverfew (*Chrysanthemum Parthenium* 'Aureum') to brighten the foreground of a groundcover planting. It would also give a lift to an otherwise all-green planting of ivy. Divide to increase.

Cultural Information: Prefers a moist soil, even boggy conditions, and may become quite invasive in such spots if not kept in check.

Ice plant; see *Succulents*

Jerusalem sage; see *Pulmonaria*

Lady's-mantle; see *Alchemilla*

Lamb's ears; see *Stachys*

Lamiastrum (lay-me-ACE-strum) yellow archangel, Easy, semievergreen to evergreen ◐ ●

Zones: 3 to 9
Height: 6 to 18 inches
Flower Color: Yellow
Characteristics: There are gardeners who will warn you not to introduce this enthusiastic creature into your landscape, but I think that is an overreaction. If accorded a spot where its tendency to romp and even cascade (over walls, for instance) is appreciated, this often-evergreen silvery-spotted groundcover can be an asset. It is more vinelike in its habit than *Lamium*, a close relative. *L. galeobdolon* 'Herman's Pride' is more clump forming than *L. g.* 'Variegatum', a zealot. In my own garden, mounds of another silvery-splashed favorite, lungwort (*Pulmonaria saccharata*), are interplanted with it.

Cultural Information: Plant it and you will be guaranteed a lifetime supply, with plenty of divisions to pass on to gardening friends. Keep *Lamiastrum* out of tightly designed garden areas or it will run through everything. Likes well-drained, moist soil. Cut back after flowering for fresh, denser growth or in fall for a neater, lusher appearance over the cold-weather months.

Lamium (LAY-mee-um) dead nettle, Easy, semievergreen to deciduous ◐ ✿

Zones: 3 to 10
Height: 6 to 18 inches
Flower Colors: White, pink
Characteristics: Showy, low-growing herbaceous groundcovers appreciated for their strongly variegated leaf markings. Foliage is marked or even nearly fully covered with silvery white areas that help brighten shady locations. *L. maculatum* 'Beacon Silver' and *L. m.* 'White Nancy' are two popular cultivars; the latter has more versatile white blooms, whereas the former's rose-pink ones can be jarring in some combinations. True to their inclusion in the mint family, they are quick, often invasive growers in many sites.

Cultural Information: Lamium likes rich, moist soil in low-light conditions. Shear after first bloom is complete to keep the plants tidy and compact. Although foliage may persist into winter in milder climates, give it a thorough pruning for best effect. Divide in spring.

Leadwort; see *Ceratostigma*

Lenten rose; see *Helleborus*

Lily, plantain; see *Hosta*

Lily of the valley; see *Convallaria*

Lilyturf; see *Liriope*

Liriope (le-RYE-oh-pee or li-ri-OH-pee) **lilyturf,** Easy, evergreen ● ○ ◗
Zones: 4 or 5 to 10
Height: 12 to 24 inches
Flower Colors: Lilac, white
Characteristics: Although they resemble small ornamental grasses, lilyturfs are actually members of the lily family. Their late-summer or fall flowers resemble those of grape hyacinth, but even without them, these evergreen plants are stalwarts of the groundcover landscape, particularly in the South and West. Lilyturf can withstand heat, humidity and even drought; it's remarkably free of ailments and pests (other than hungry slugs and rabbits). Many a southern plantation walkway is lined with *Liriope*; countless live oaks and pecan trees are encircled with the stuff, too, and numerous warm-zone office parks and other institutional plantings serve it up as main fare. The home gardener can easily avoid such monotonous use of the plain green forms, though, because there are better options: In the best ornamental species, *L. muscari* (about 18 inches high with arcing, strappy leaves), try 'Silvery Sunproof', which can tolerate sunny exposures, or 'Variegata', which prefers part shade. On a smaller scale, *L. spicata* (8 to 12 inches, all green with finer-textured leaves), looks more like large blades of grass; it can be invasive in some settings, but tolerates low light condition better than *L. muscari*. *L. muscari*, in particular, is handsome along paths or at the foreground of stands of bamboo. Frequently confused with *Ophiopogon* (below).
Cultural Information: Although fully evergreen in all but the coldest climates, *L. spicata*, in particular, appreciates a haircut in late winter or early spring, which will stimulate a flush of fresh foliage. In northern areas, cold, dry winter weather can burn foliage of *L. muscari*, which can be given the same treatment or simply selectively tidied up with scissors. Fleshy-rooted and easily increased by division.

Lungwort; see *Pulmonaria*

Lysimachia (ly-sim-AK-ee-uh) **moneywort** or **creeping jennie,** Easy, evergreen to semievergreen ◗ ● ⬚
Zones: 4 to 10
Height: 1 to 2 inches
Flower Color: Yellow
Characteristics: L. nummularia's long runners root at each joint, giving it fast, easy footholds along its ever-widening path. It

Liriope muscari *'Variegata'*

is especially good for carpeting stream banks and edges of ponds, because it is a real moisture lover. The form to grow is *L. n.* 'Aurea', a golden-leaved cultivar, which creates a mat of yellow foliage that can light up the ground fast.
Cultural Information: Moist, but not swampy, soil in a partly shady exposure is moneywort's preference; the golden form is particularly shy of direct sun, but can turn a pale green if grown in too dark an exposure.

Mazus (MAY-zus) **mazus,** Easy, evergreen to semievergreen ○ ◑
Zones: 4 to 10
Height: 1 inch
Flower Colors: Blue-purple, white
Characteristics: Mazus reptans is an enthusiastic grower, but one on the shortest scale. A potential lawn substitute that can withstand light foot traffic, it remains evergreen in warmer zones, and boasts late-spring flowers, too. Fine in the cracks in a path or patio.

Lysimachia nummularia

Mazus reptans

Moss

Sagina subulata 'Aurea'

Ophiopogon
planiscipus
'Nigrescens', *planted
in cracks*

Cultural Information: A sunny or partly shady spot with adequate soil moisture is to mazus's liking. In good garden soil, it will run rampant. Divide to increase, although *Mazus* increases on its own just fine.

Mock strawberry; see Strawberry Look-Alikes

Mondo grass; see Ophiopogon

Moneywort; see Lysimachia

Moss and Mosslike Plants, Moderate, evergreen, many native ● ◐

Zones: Various
Height: 1/16 inch to 2 feet
Characteristics: I learned to appreciate moss in the John P. Humes Japanese Stroll Garden on Long Island, New York, where curator Stephen Morrell cultivates the stuff with a love that rosarians give their most beloved hybrid tea roses. As a groundcover, moss lends a depth and texture to the shady garden that no other material can; in conjunction with stone, it is dramatic, a contrast of soft and hard, of delicate and indestructible. Morrell's tricks for nurturing moss include a periodic spray of buttermilk diluted with water, and regular misting. Moss cannot withstand drying out.

The world of mosses is vast, but as they are rarely grown as a nursery crop, their identification is virtually unknown to gardeners. The lower-growing forms, like cushions of velvet, can be planted as accents or entire carpets, and are good on gentle slopes. They will tolerate only light foot traffic, so if you want

to plant a moss lawn, be sure to install stepping-stones along the principal routes.

Irish and Scotch mosses (*Sagina subulata*) are not true mosses, despite their common names. *Arenaria verna* is another very similar moss look-alike. Both are more commonly grown as garden plants than true mosses, growing to about 4 inches. The Scotch is a more golden green, the Irish, pure green. In mid- to late summer, they are covered with tiny white flowers (true mosses do not flower, but reproduce by spores). Good in crevices in steps, walks and patios.

Cultural Information: True mosses like shade to part shade and moisture; they are frequently found living in association with rotting trees and other decaying organic material of the forest floor, where conditions are acidic. *Sagina* and *Arenaria* like more fertile, well-drained garden soil, and will not grow in deep shade. Increase all by division.

Nettle, dead; see Lamium

Oconee bells; see Shortia

Ophiopogon (oh-fee-oh-POE-gon) mondo grass, Easy, evergreen ● ○

Zones: 6 or 7 to 10
Height: 6 to 12 inches
Flower Colors: White, lilac
Characteristics: Grassy, evergreen foliage plant frequently mistaken for *Liriope* (see above); *Ophiopogon* fruits are blue, not black, and its flowers are borne lower down than *Liriope*'s toward the foliage. Mondo grass is less hardy, but it does come

in an incredible "black" foliage form, *O. planiscapus* 'Nigrescens', or 'Arabicus', outstanding when harmonized with the coloring of Japanese painted fern, or contrasted with yellow-foliage hostas, creeping jennie and the ivy called *Hedera Helix* 'Buttercup', or the fresh, pale green of many ferns. *O. japonicus*, at about a foot tall, is a handsome dark green ground-cover requiring little care.
Cultural Information: Durable, easy plants for warmer zones, basically carefree. May need some early spring cleanup if winter damage occurs; cut out messy foliage. Divide to propagate.

Opuntia; see *Succulents*

Ornamental Grasses

Over the last five or so years, gardeners have heard the praises of ornamental grasses. Botanical gardens have installed grass gardens; they have been touted in magazine articles and whole books and catalogs, and local nurseries have begun to stock them with greater regularity. But few gardeners have really explored the grasses in their own backyards, other than as an accent or specimen in an existing flower border.

The category we loosely term ornamental grasses actually includes some plants that aren't grasses at all, botanically speaking, but simply grasslike: *Ophiopogon* (see page 60), *Liriope* (see page 59), the sedges (*Carex*) and rushes (*Juncus*), for example. Bamboos, which are in fact grass relatives, are also sometimes lumped into this vast

assemblage; unlike the others, they have woody stems.

Among the true grasses and these look-alikes, there is much diversity. Visually, grasses can be as tidy and mounded as the fescues (*Festuca*) or running every which way, carpeting the ground enthusiastically in the manner of blue lyme grass (*Elymus arenarius*) or ribbon grass (*Phalaris arundinacea picta*). There are tall, strongly vertical grasses best for punctuating designs, like ravennae grass (*Erianthus ravennae*). Perhaps the most graceful of all is *Pennisetum*, commonly known as fountain grass for the way it seems to spill out of itself.

The word *grass* certainly evokes an image of closely mowed stretches of green, but ornamental grasses represent an enormously wide segment of the gardener's palette. Yes, there is every manner of green, but also shades of silver and blue in fescue and lyme grass; clear red in bloodgrass (*Imperata cylindrica rubra*), the purple hue of *Panicum virgatum* 'Heavy Metal', and others with stripes or margins of white, cream or yellow. Seed heads, borne late in the season, may add touches of pink, bronze, gold and even black to the picture; then, as foliage begins to fade, even the plainest green grass passes through warming tones of beige, gold and cinnamon—the amber waves of grain. Left in place, these faced echoes of the season will catch the snow and rustle in the winter breeze. Birds will feast on the seed heads and take shelter, too.

There are grasses for wet spots (*Carex* species, *Phalaris*

arundinacea and *Molinia caerulea*, to name a few) and others that display great drought tolerance, such as *Elymus arenarius*, a fine choice for seaside locations with quick-draining, sandy soil. Most grasses want a sunny exposure, although *Pha-*

Calimagrotis *species*

Phalaris arundinacea picta

Miscanthus sinensis, *rear, and* Pennisetum alopecuroides, *foreground*

Oxalis *(redwood sorrel)*

Phlox divaricata

laris arundinacea picta and northern sea oats (*Chasmanthium latifolium*) are two that will take light shade.

As a rule, plant or transplant grasses in the spring so that they have ample time to settle in before frost. Cut them down in late winter as new growth begins to show, without damaging emerging shoots. In the Conservatory Garden in Central Park, New York City, curator Sarah Price makes these exceptions: She doesn't cut down *Helictotrichon* at all, but grooms it by teasing out brown foliage by hand when necessary. She cuts ribbon grass (*Phalaris arundinacea picta*) down in late winter, and then in half in mid-June to early July so that it stays fuller and more tidy looking. Other tips from the Conservatory Garden: Northern sea oats will look better if given a bit of support, in the form of a stake or grow-through ring. The big *Miscanthus* species are also staked.

Oxalis (ox-AL-lis) **wood sorrel, oxalis,** Easy, semievergreen to deciduous, some natives ○ ◐

Zones: Various
Height: 3 to 12 inches
Flower Colors: White, pink, red, yellow
Characteristics: A family of plants variously produced from tubers, rhizomes or fleshy roots, whose leaves, sour to the taste, usually resemble those of clover. The foliage comes in various colors and sizes, some of it marked attractively. Even those that are not hardy in a particular zone can be used effectively as bedding plants, treated as annuals; the cultivar listed commercially as *Oxalis triangularis* (Zones 8 to 10), with its two-tone purple leaves and pink flowers, has been so used in recent seasons. Two indigenous species, the American wood sorrel (*O. montana*, Zone 4, of Canada and the Northeast and northern Midwest) and redwood sorrel (*O. oregona*, Zone 7, a native of the coastal forests of California and Oregon) are appropriate for naturalizing in wild, shady locales. They combine well with ferns.
Cultural Information: For the most part, oxalis likes a partly shady locale and adequate moisture, although many can withstand a summertime dry spell. Divide to increase.

Pearly everlasting; see ***Anaphalis***

Phlox (flocks) **phlox,** Easy, semievergreen to deciduous, many native ○ ◐ 💧

Zones: 3 to 9
Height: 3 to 12 inches
Flower Colors: Pink, white, lilac, blue
Characteristics: Among the genius *Phlox* are a number of low-growing perennials that offer creeping, mounded masses of color and persistent foliage for a variety of environments. Moss pink (*P. subulata*) produces a woody mat of needlelike, evergreen growth and blooms in pink, white or mauve; *P. s.* 'Coral Eye' is white with a coral center, and reblooms. Place in a rock garden, where it will form large sheets of color even on slopes, or another sunny spot. Wild sweet william (*P. divaricata*, about 1 foot high) is a shadier woodland creature, the flowers of which are blue or white ('Fuller's White' is a fine form). With spring bulbs, *P. divaricata* is beautiful; as a foreground to emerging ferns and hostas, it is outstanding when in flower, then turns over the show gracefully to those next in line. It also teams well with yellow-flowered corydalis (*Corydalis lutea*) and bleeding heart (*Dicentra spectabilis*), with pink or white blooms.
Cultural Information: Cutting *P. subulata* back by half after flowering will ward off the scraggly, leggy look that sometimes occurs otherwise. It tolerates a leaner soil than does *P. divaricata* and is more drought tolerant. Divide, or reproduce from cuttings.

Plantain lily; see ***Hosta***

Prickly pear; see ***Succulents***

Primrose; see *Primula*

Primula (PRIM-yew-la) **primrose,** Moderate, semievergreen to deciduous ◑ ⚘
Zones: 3 or 5 to 8 or 9, depending on species
Height: 6 to 24 inches
Flower Colors: All
Characteristics: Primula makes a charming groundcover for the moist, partly shady garden, particularly beautiful when it flowers in spring. Many of the flowers are brightly colored and borne high above the low rosettes of foliage. The familiar *P. polyantha* hybrids are very early bloomers and among the hardiest of all, to Zone 3. Good with spring bulbs, their foliage is almost evergreen. The species *P. japonica* is relatively easy and inclined to create large colonies; hardy only to Zone 5, it likes wet spots. *P. j.* 'Millar's Crimson' is a showy cultivar. Plant primroses in masses in naturalistic settings for best effect. Fine with ferns, astilbes and irises, brilliant along stream banks and in low, moist spots in the dappled light of a woodland.
Cultural Information: Humus-rich, moisture-retentive soils are a must for primroses. Even where they are fully hardy, heaving can be a problem with these shallow-rooted plants, so apply a winter mulch where repeated freezes and thaws are common. Summer heat is also tough on most of them; they are not for hot, dry regions of the country, but numerous species can be grown in the Pacific Northwest and in portions of New England, among other places. Cool, moist conditions are the key to suc-cess. Divide after flowering to increase, or grow from seed.

Pulmonaria (pul-mo-NAY-ree-uh) **lungwort, Jerusalem sage,** Easy, deciduous ◑ ●
Zones: 3 to 9
Height: 6 to 8 inches
Flower Colors: Purplish pink, white, blue
Characteristics: A family of co-operative but not invasive ground-covering perennials that are quick to increase in height and produce seedlings, too. The main attraction of lungwort is its silvery- or white-splotched leaves, which are hairy textured. I think that they are quite beautiful and bring the illusion of sparkles of light into the partial shade below deciduous trees and large shrubs. The cultivars of *P. saccharata* are a showy lot, and quite diverse; *P. s.* 'Mrs. Moon' and *P. s.* 'Alba' are well marked with white; the leaves of *P. s.* 'Roy Davidson' are slender and evenly spotted with silver. Try assembling a collection to discern how you like them together; I think they are at their best in one another's company.
Cultural Information: You may think you have lost a lungwort when you transplant it; it will wilt and shrivel up so pathetically. Be sure to give it a deep watering, cut off any flowers and wait. These are not such delicate creatures after all. Lungwort's only drawback is an inclination to mildew late in the season. Divide to propagate, or sow seed.

Pussytoes; see *Antennaria*

Rock cress; see *Arabis*

Primula japonica

Rose, Christmas; see *Helleborus*

Rose, Lenten; see *Helleborus*

Sage, Jerusalem; see *Pulmonaria*

Pulmonaria saccharata

Sanguinaria (sang-gwon-AIR-ee-uh) **bloodroot,** Moderate, deciduous, native ● ◑

Zones: 3 to 9
Height: 6 inches
Flower Color: White
Characteristics: S. canadensis, the native wildflower called bloodroot, is slow to multiply, but eventually spreads to create colonies. Its unusual foliage is very attractive, but becomes tattered in mid- to late summer and then goes dormant. Appropriate naturalized in the wild

Sanguinaria canadensis

Saxifraga stolonifera

garden, where its tendency to disappear early will not be so problematic, or interplanted with pachysandra or other more common groundcovers to add foliar contrast and the attraction of white, early-spring blooms. A double-flowered form brings high prices in catalogs. Digging in bloodroot would be a great way to much improve the look of a large bed of otherwise dull, evergreen groundcover, provided the site is shady and not too dry. The common name comes from the orange-red color of the sap, used by Native Americans as war paint and dye.
Cultural Information: Woodsy, moist soil and a shady site are bloodroot's favorites. Divide when dormant to increase.

Saxifraga (SAX-if-rag-a) **saxifrage,** Easy to moderate, many evergreen, some native ◑ ○
Zones: Various
Height: 3 to 36 inches
Flower Colors: White, pink, red, yellow
Characteristics: Probably the most familiar face from this enormous genus of plants is that of the strawberry begonia or mother-of-thousands (S. stolonifera), a fine groundcover in shady exposures of our warmer zones (6 to 10) and a traditional houseplant elsewhere. Its rounded leaves are silver-veined above and reddish on their undersides, and the plants expand as strawberries do, sending out numerous baby plantlets on the ends of wiry runners. This Asian native is sometimes listed as S. sarmentosa and grows about 6 inches high. The foliage of London pride saxifrage (S. ×urbium) is also about 6 inches

high, forming evergreen rosettes topped by an effusion of white or pink flowers in spring. There are Saxifraga whose appearance is positively mosslike, forming tiny tufted mounds, such as the S. ×Arendsii hybrids with names like 'Snow Carpet' and 'Flower Carpet'; others look more like succulents. Generally, both of these are better suited to the rockery, however, than for massing as groundcover. At the other end of the size scale is an American native, the Pennsylvania saxifrage, a green-flowered biennial growing to about 3 feet.
Cultural Information: There are saxifrages for shade and sun; most require moist but well-drained, alkaline soil. The strawberry begonia is among the least fussy of the lot, although it wants protection from hot, midday sun and ample soil moisture. Propagate by seed, division and runners.

Saxifrage; see ***Saxifraga***

Sedum (SEE-dum) **sedum, stonecrop,** Easy, semievergreen ○ ◑
Zones: 3 to 9
Height: 2 to 24 inches
Flower Colors: White, yellow, pink, rose
Characteristics: The large and somewhat confusing genus of succulents called Sedum is a very useful one for gardeners who appreciate plants that practically take care of themselves. Many have a long season of interest, notably S. spectabile 'Autumn Joy', which emerges from a hen-and-chicken stage in earliest spring up to a green broccoli stage by early summer, colors up to pinkish red in fall

and then stands stiffly in its dried seed-head state to catch the snow in winter. It grows about 18 to 24 inches, is excellent for drying when the flower heads first turn color, and will also grow in part shade if given some support, because it will be less sturdy there. Other favorites include S. 'Vera Jamison' and S. 'Ruby Glow', similar-looking plants about 8 inches high; the former's leaves are more purplish, the latter's, marked with dark red. Their flowers are pink to red; plant them together for a same-but-different juxtaposition. S. kamtschaticum 'Variegatum', 6 to 12 inches high, has leaves edged in creamy white and yellow flowers—very showy. Whereas S. s. 'Autumn Joy' has erect stems, the last three have sprawling habits. A gardener in need of a boost in confidence need only plant a handful of low-growing Sedum acre to have a bumper crop in short order—great for filling in tough spots where no other plant seems inclined to cooperate. Golden flowers in late spring (many sedums bloom in late summer) are a bonus on this 2-inch species. Another small member of the genus, S. spurium, is slightly taller, and is at least as enthusiastic as S. acre. I have buried bits of it inadvertently under a wheelbarrow-load of topsoil, only to have it creep up and out and try to cover the whole mound. The most popular S. spurium cultivar is 'Dragon's Blood', whose foliage is tinged with purple-red. The long-lasting flowers are red, too.

Because of their succulence, many sedum possess sculptural qualities and, therefore, contrast dramatically with most other plants. The low-growers are best as edgers and in rockeries; taller varieties, such as S. s. 'Autumn Joy', are most dramatic when massed.

Cultural Information: Sedums are at their best in well-drained, sunny locations, but I have seen many different species grow in shady spots, too. Flowering will not be as good and stems will be floppier, but you have to work to find a spot that sedum will not at least try to grow in. Poor soil seems to pose no problem for sedum either, particularly the smaller species, which are happy in sand-filled cracks in a stone path. Propagation is easier than easy; break off bits of stem at almost any time and simply stick them elsewhere and you will have more. Division is equally simple. I have cut flowering stems of various sedums for indoor arrangements and had them root themselves in the vase of water or even when hung upside down while air drying; that is how vigorous these plants are.

Shortia (SHORT-ee-uh) **oconee bells,** moderate, evergreen, native. ● ◗ ⚱
Zones: 4 to 8
Height: 8 inches
Flower Color: White
Characteristics: Shortia galacifolia, found in the moist woodlands of the Carolinas, is a shade-loving groundcover with glossy, evergreen foliage that bronzes up in winter. Dainty white flowers are produced in springtime. Great in the shade of rhododendron, because *Shortia* likes a similarly acid soil. May be confused with *Galax,* to which its species name gives credit.

Cultural Information: Give it a home in a moist, highly organic soil of an acid nature. *Shortia* may be slow to establish and appreciates a light dressing of rotted oak leaves in fall. Divide to increase.

Siberian bugloss; see ***Brunnera***

Snow-in-summer; see ***Cerastium***

Sorrel, wood; see ***Oxalis***

Speedwell; see ***Veronica***

Stachys (STA-chys) **lamb's ears,** Easy, semievergreen to evergreen ○ ◗
Zones: 4 to 8
Height: 1 foot
Flower Color: Usually purple
Characteristics: I cannot pass a mat of lamb's ears (*S. byzantina,* sometimes listed as *S. lantana*), without bending to pet its thickly felted, silvery leaves. How can such a furry thing be plant, not animal? This is certainly one of

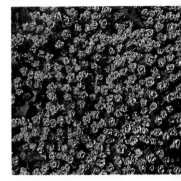

Sedum dasyphyllum

Shortia *species*

Stachys byzantina

Waldsteinia *species*

Sedum *and*
Sempervivum

Fragaria *species*

the finest plants that I know of for covering the ground in sunny spots. Its combined attributes of leaf texture and color draw the eye to them, and I even like its peculiar flowers, which many gardeners prefer to cut off. (Save yourself the trouble and grow the nonflowering cultivar *S. b.* 'Silver Carpet'.) Let it sprawl at the feet of purple foliage plants, in front of a purple-leaved sand cherry shrub (*Prunus* × *cistena*), for instance, or with the annual herbs purple basil and *Perilla frutescens*, a coleus look-alike used in Japanese cuisine. For a same-but-different statement in silver, plant with the delicate, lacy foliage of *Artemisia*. Excellent dried, too.

Cultural Information: Stachys, like most silver-leaved plants, is a sun lover. It appreciates well-drained soil. Hot, humid spells can take their toll on *Stachys*, and the foliage will rot out in such conditions. In climates where midsummer produces such effects, plants may rebound in the fall. Don't water overhead in heat spells, as this will induce the same effect as a humid southern summertime. Clean up by teasing out faded leaves several times during the season, and particularly at winter's end. Divide to increase.

Stonecrop; see ***Sedum***

Strawberry, barren; see ***Strawberry Look-Alikes***

Strawberry Look-Alikes
It can be quite confusing to keep the cast straight when it comes to the strawberries and strawberry look-alikes that are used as groundcovers. All of the following have the classic strawberry habit of producing offsets on runners, and all have strawberry-like blooms, although many are yellow in flower, not white like those of a true strawberry.

DUCHESNEA (doo-SHAYS-nea) or mock strawberry, hardy from Zones 3 to 10, grows to about 6 inches. Yellow flowers, followed by little "strawberries," are borne in spring or summer. Evergreen and a fast grower, it can be mown in late winter to promote fresh foliage. *D. indica* is widely naturalized in the United States, but is not a native. Grow in sun to shade.

FRAGARIA (frag-AIR-ee-uh), the wild strawberry, includes several species of native plants, all true strawberries with white flowers. *F. chiloensis*, Zones 5 to 10, grows to less than 1 foot in sun or part shade. Persistent foliage bronzes or reddens in winter. Mow to freshen large plantings, as with *Duchesnea.*

WALDSTEINIA (wald-STY-knee-uh), the barren strawberry, is an American native, hailing from the Northeast and southern Canada. Grow *W. fragarioides* in sun to part shade, even in dry, lean soils. Its leaves bronze up in cold weather.

All three can be easily increased by division; all are best used in masses in naturalistic settings, as they are not formal plants.

Strawberry, mock; see *Strawberry Look-Alikes*

Strawberry, wild; see *Strawberry Look-Alikes*

Succulents

Excellent drainage and sunny exposures are basic preferences shared by these genera of fleshy-leaved plants, which provide sculptural forms to the garden, often year 'round.

Most (not including the single species of cactus listed below) have their leaves arranged in the familiar rosette structure, at least in early spring.

Possibilities for groundcover include the following.

AGAVE (ag-AH-vay), most of them hardy only to Zone 10, usually have gray-green leaves (sometimes variegated with stripes of cream) that are pointed and sharp-toothed. They range in height from 1 foot or so to about 15 feet. Probably the most familiar is the century plant (*A. americana*, about 3 feet).

ALOE (AL-oh), a genus that includes *A. vera*, source of the gel used to promote healing in skin injuries, includes plants

of many heights, from less than 1 foot to those with the stature of trees. Leaves are frequently mottled or banded in darker colors than the grayish green and greens of the plain forms. They are drought tolerant and very useful in such climates as that of southern California, hardy to about Zone 9.

ECHEVERIA (esh-eve-EER-ee-uh), Mexican natives, ranging in height from just an inch or so to a few feet tall, are principally grown in Zones 9 and 10. Most have gray-green leaves arranged in rosettes, and their flowers are long lasting.

ICE PLANTS, blanketing the tops of many coastal California cliffsides with often-electric shades of purple, pink, orange, red, yellow and white, are ac-

tually members of a half-dozen or so genera, all of them formerly grouped under the name *Mesembryanthemum.* Their flowers are numerous and daisylike. Those of *Lampranthus* appear in midwinter or spring, for example; *Drosanthemum* blooms in late spring. Most ice plants are hardy in Zones 9 and 10; some are slightly more cold tolerant. All are durable charac-

Echeveria

Ice plants

Opuntia humifusa

Tiarella cordifolia

Symphytum grandiflorum

ters asking little of the gardener, the toughest of the lot content to make their home in pure sand.

OPUNTIA (oh-PUN-tea-uh), a cactus commonly called prickly pear, includes some sprawling American natives like *O. humifusa austrina*, hardy as cold as Zone 5 or 6. It makes an excellent groundcover for out-of-the-way areas of seaside gardens, and will happily clamber over rocky walls. Yellow flowers are borne in midsummer. Because they are very prickly they are somewhat hard to handle, but this same quality makes *Opuntia* a good choice for setting boundaries you do not wish crossed.

SEDUM (see page 64), which in the case of most species dies back to near the ground at season's end, is not a desert plant at all; neither are the most commonly cultivated *Sempervivum* (sem-purr-VIV-um) or hens and chickens or houseleeks. The lat-

ter are hardy from Zones 3 or 4 to 8, and evergreen, requiring only the tiniest amounts of soil to survive; they are a classic sight in craggy old stone walls, but happy in the garden, too.

Sweet woodruff; see *Galium*

Symphytum (SIM-fit-um) comfrey, Easy, deciduous. ○ ◑

Zones: 3 to 9
Height: 12 to 24 inches
Flower Colors: Blue, pink, red, white
Characteristics: The smaller members of the comfrey clan are somewhat coarse groundcovers, but cooperative and fine at suppressing weeds. Look for the form of *S. grandiflorum* 'Variegatum' which will tolerate shade even in dry spots, although it prefers even soil moisture like the rest of the comfreys. A redflowered form, *S. rubrum*, is another good groundcover choice that tolerates dry shade and is somewhat slower growing.
Cultural Information: Comfreys are robust growers. Cut back after flowering to keep the plants tidy and compact. Easily propagated by divisions of the fleshy roots.

Tiarella (tea-uh-RELL-uh) foamflower, Easy, evergreen or semievergreen, native ◑ ● 🌱

Zones: 3 to 9
Height: 6 to 8 inches
Flower Colors: White, pale pink
Characteristics: *T. cordifolia* is probably the most commonly grown foamflower, a charming little woodland native with maplelike leaves. *T. wherryi* is a tidier clump former than its stoloniferous cousin. Both are longblooming; you will understand

the common name when you see *Tiarella* in bloom, a froth of white. The foamflower leaves are somewhat hairy and have patterns of darker veination, which sometimes go bronze or purplish in winter. With the variegated ribbon grass (*Phalaris arundinacea picta*), another plant at its best in part shade, it is stunning; a mixed planting of semievergreen to evergreen woodlanders such as *Tiarella*, Christmas fern and wild ginger would also provide a good contrast of foliar forms.

Cultural Information: *Tiarella* likes the moist, organic soil of the woodland environment from which it hails. Don't let the planting dry out. If deadheaded, it will rebloom. Divide to increase, or grow from seed.

Tovara (toe-VAH-rah) **tovara,**
Easy, deciduous, native ◐ ○
Zones: 5 to 8
Height: 2 to 3 feet
Flower Color: Reddish
Characteristics: Why don't we see *Tovara virginiana* in every garden? The variegated forms in particular, among them 'Variegata' (green-and-cream splotched leaves) and 'Painter's Palette' (green, cream and reddish leaves), are incredibly showy, and it is an easy plant to cultivate. That it is actually classified along with the pernicious knotweed as a *Polygonum* botanically (although retaining the name *Tovara* among horticulturists) hints at its enthusiastic habit of growth, as does the fact that it is a native American plant, indigenous to the eastern and central states. The only plausible explanation for its absence from

most gardens is that you really have to look for it in catalog listings and nurseries, then snatch it up when it is available, although that is certain to change as more and more gardeners get a look. It is relatively tall compared with many other groundcovers highlighted here and is covered in a profusion of leaves so it is almost shrubby in appearance. Among flower arrangers, it is prized for its foliage, and also for the strange if insignificant flowers, like strands of red wire. Dare I suggest planting it with another variegate nearby, such as an ornamental grass? I think it would be stunning.

Cultural Information: *Tovara* will spread lustily in good garden soil, particularly when it is moist. Leaves are apt to burn in windy spots or where the midday sun is too intense, so a protected site may be preferable.

Vancouveria (van-koo-VEER-e-uh) **American barrenwort,**
Easy, evergreen or deciduous, native ◐ ◓
Zones: 5 to 8
Height: 10 to 12 inches
Flower Colors: White, yellow
Characteristics: Reminiscent of *Epimedium*, to which it is related, *Vancouveria* is an ideal groundcover for the woodland floor. Where happy, as in its native Pacific Northwest, it lends a mounded, ferny effect, but it will not tolerate the heat and dryness so common to summer in much of the nation. *Vancouveria* blooms, usually producing white flowers, in late spring. *V. hexandra*, the fastest grower and toughest of the lot, is de-

Tovara virginianum *'Variegata'*

ciduous; *V. chrysantha* (with yellow flowers) and *V. planipetala* are evergreen, but somewhat harder to get going.

Cultural Information: Moist soil of an acidic nature is preferred by *Vancouveria*, although *V. hexandra* will tolerate periods of dryness if they are not combined with great heat. Divide to increase.

Vancouveria hexandra

Veronica (ver-ON-ick-ah)
speedwell, Easy, deciduous
○ ◑
Zones: 4 to 9
Height: 3 to 48 inches
Flower Colors: Blue, white, purple

Characteristics: There are many speedwells enjoyed in the flower garden for their spiky inflorescences, and a few that can be used as groundcovers, whose habit is more prostrate. *V. incana* is one such candidate, with hairy silver foliage and blue flowers

Veronica oltensis

(12 to 18 inches), or try nonflowering *V. i.* 'Silver Slippers' for a handsome mat of gray. *V. prostrata* is shorter, with soft gray-green foliage and blue flowers. It can be pruned if the matlike foliage gets out of hand. *V. repens*, a charming little speedwell about 3 inches high that is suited to cracks in pavers and withstands some trampling, has become an invasive lawn weed in some regions.
Cultural Information: Speedwells are easy plants asking average soil. They bloom best in full sun, but can tolerate a bit less if asked. Divide or grow from seed.

Viola (vy-OH-la) **violet,** Easy, most evergreen to semievergreen, some native ○ ◑
Zones: Varies
Height: 1 to 12 inches
Flower Colors: White, purple, pink, red, orange, yellow, bicolors
Characteristics: This is the genus that includes both the perennial violets and also the pansies and violas we grow as annual bedding plants. The latter prefer more light than the former, generally speaking. All make good groundcovers, although the annuals are grown more for their long-lasting flower show. The perennials have more delicate flowers but their handsome and enduring foliage, roughly heart- or kidney-shaped, makes them better choices in many situations. The roundleaf violet (*V. rotundifolia*) with yellow flowers, and sweet white violet (*V. blanda*, 2 inches, likes moist soil) are two such choices; Labrador violet, *V. labradorica*, 1 to 4 inches, another moisture lover, produces mauve blossoms.

Viola tricolor 'Helen Mount'

All three species are natives, and hardy as cold as Zone 3 and up to 7 or 8, best used in a wild garden or massed as groundcovers for a woodsy setting. The tufted pansy (*V. cornuta*, Zones 5 to 9) is a profuse and long bloomer; try the Burpee introduction 'Princess Blue', with 1-inch flowers. The plants are just 6 inches high but wide spreading. Johnny-jump-ups like *Viola tricolor* 'Helen Mount' are among the brightest and cheeriest of all.
Cultural Information: Rich, moist soil and filtered light are what the perennials like; grow the annual bedders in sunnier spots for best flowering. All *Violas* do best in the cool portions of the season; the annuals will peter out in midsummer heat in some areas, and the perennials will slow down, too. Most are prodigious self sowers; many of the perennials can also be increased by division.

Violet; see *Viola*

Waldsteinia; see *Strawberry Look-Alikes*

Wall cress; see *Arabis*

Wandflower; see *Galax*

Wild ginger; see *Asarum*

Wild strawberry; see *Strawberry Look-Alikes*

Wood sorrel; see *Oxalis*

Woodruff, sweet; see *Galium*

Yellow archangel; see *Lamiastrum*

WOODY GROUNDCOVERS

Alleghany spurge; see *Pachysandra*

Arctostaphylos (ark-toe-STAFF-il-los) **bearberry, manzanita,** Easy, evergreen, native ○ ◐ ◗

Zones: 2 to 10
Height: 6 to 12 inches
Flower Colors: White, pink
Characteristics: A. *uva-ursi*, native throughout the nation, is prized for its durability even in heat and sandy soils or at seaside locations. Its small evergreen leaves bronze up in cool weather; after the waxy flowers fade, red berries form that are attractive to birds. Related plants grown as groundcovers in many warm western zones include those commonly known as manzanitas (the fruit do indeed look like small apples, which is what the name translates to). Some recommended ones are Little Sur manzanita (*A. Edmundsii*, less than 2 feet) and *A.* 'Emerald Carpet', about 1 foot high. These are far less cold hardy, only to about Zone 7. All of the *Arctostaphylos* clan are recommended for use on slopes and hillsides.
Cultural Information: The *Arctostaphylos* relatives like well-drained, even sandy, soil ideally somewhat acid in nature. They are drought-tolerant plants, easy to grow but not as easy to propagate, so start with nursery-grown plantlets for best results.

Baccharis (BAK-kar-iss) **coyote brush,** Easy, evergreen, native ○ ◐ ◗

Zones: 7 to 10
Height: 8 to 24 inches
Flower Color: Off-white

Characteristics: B. *pilularis*, dwarf coyote brush, is a drought-tolerant, evergreen shrub that makes a good choice in the Southwest and West, owing to its coastal California heritage. Although the flowers are nothing to speak of, coyote brush is good-looking year 'round, with somewhat mounded, dense foliage of either dark green (ask for the cultivar 'Twin Peaks') or light green (try 'Pigeon Point', a faster grower). Seedless male plants are preferred, and far less messy; check that you are buying males only.
Cultural Information: The dwarf form of coyote brush is tolerant of many soils, including sandy ones, and can even tolerate desert heat. In late winter or early spring, prune out branches that tend to arc upward to maintain neat, low appearance. Spider mites may be a problem. Purchase plants grown from cuttings of male stock plants.

Bearberry; see *Arctostaphylos*

Blackberry, flowering; see ***Rubus***

Bramble; see ***Rubus***

Brush, coyote; see ***Baccharis***

Calluna (kah-LOON-uh) **heather,** Moderate, evergreen ○ ◐

Zones: 5 to 9
Height: 3 to 18 inches
Flower Colors: Purple, pink, white

Arctostaphylos uva-ursi

San Francisco landscape architect Ron Lutsko uses the soft mounded habit of dwarf coyote brush (Baccharis pilularis 'Twin Peaks') to offset the hard lines of a swimming pool.

Calluna *and* Erica *species*

Characteristics: A hillside of heather is a thing to behold in late summer, when it is covered with clusters of flowers that seem to form a hazy cloud of subtle color. The flowers are not just long lasting, but are also fine for cutting and drying. A mixed planting of *Calluna*, *Erica carnea* (heath, a similar-looking plant with springtime flowers) and low-growing juniper would make an excellent four-season showing. Heathers will perform best in sunny spots, and also benefit from some protection from winter wind, as they are prone to tip burn and dessication. They are somewhat slow growing and not exceptionally drought tolerant, preferring their roots to take hold in moist soil. Don't settle for only green-leaved heathers. 'Gold Haze' is one cultivar that offers golden foliage all season (some gold-leaved heathers take on orange or red fall color as a bonus); 'J. H. Hamilton' and 'White Lawn' are among the many that turn to a handsome shade of plum in the cold-weather months. Those varieties whose leaves are coated with fine white hairs for a silvery effect are equally useful in designing a mass planting.

Cultural Information: Grow heather in well-drained soil that is neither too rich nor too dry. Do not feed these plants with a nitrogen-rich fertilizer; that is precisely what they do not want. The addition of shredded, rotted oak leaves and peat moss will do much to promote the ideal environment, as heathers desire a pH on the acid side (6 or lower). Sandy soil, which is naturally well drained, can be amended this way to make an ideal environment for growing heathers. Prune hard by shearing in early spring to remove winterkill; this process also improves flowering. Provide a year-'round mulch of pine needles, shredded pine bark or shredded oak leaves. Plants can be increased by cuttings or by layering (make a partial cut in the underside of stems, then bury the cuts in the soil until they take root and can be severed from the mother plant), which is also a good way to revive older plants.

Candytuft, perennial; see *Iberis*

Ceanothus (see-uh-KNOW-thus) **ceanothus, wild lilac,** Easy, semievergreen to evergreen, native ○ ◑
Zones: 7 to 10
Height: 18 inches to 30 feet
Flower Color: Blue
Characteristics: There are two good groundcover candidates among the *Ceanothus* clan, a genus of mostly taller, showy springtime bloomers that are fast-growing and durable. As their common names give away, these are coastal plants from the West, and they are best used in large-scale plantings since even a single plant has a great spread. The Point Reyes ceanothus (*C. gloriosus*) may reach only 18 inches high, but it may be ten times as wide at

Ceanothus *species*

maturity; 'Anchor Bay' has very dense foliage that thwarts weeds. The Carmel creeper (*C. griseus horizontalis*) is up to a foot taller, and 6 to 12 feet across; the variety 'Yankee Point' is very floriferous. *Ceanothus* are good bank holders, helpful in spots where erosion is a problem. They are also tolerant of dry periods and salt air.

Cultural Information: Full sun and well-drained soil are preferred by *Ceanothus*. Cut out dead or damaged wood in early spring. Particularly when they are grown in a garden setting, where they are watered regularly, *Ceanothus* may suffer from root rot, because in their native habitat they are accustomed to long dry periods during the heat of summertime. Keep this in mind and don't water established plantings unnecessarily; let them get by on nature's offerings as much as possible.

Cinquefoil; see *Potentilla*

Cotoneaster (koh-toe-knee-ASS-ter) cotoneaster, Easy, deciduous or evergreen ○ ◖

Zones: 4 or 5 to 7 or 8
Height: 6 inches to 15 feet
Flower Colors: White, pink
Characteristics: Although frequently planted in an uninspired manner, *Cotoneaster* are attractive shrubs whose berries in mostly fire-engine shades cannot be overlooked, even from quite a distance. Just ask the birds, who are only too happy to stop in and sample them. The branching habit is usually fountainlike or arching, and this adds greatly to the plant's appeal, making it a good choice

for spilling over retaining walls and otherwise softening hard edges. However, when *Cotoneaster* is planted in too-tight quarters, and requires heavy pruning to be kept in bounds, this grace is quickly lost to the shears. Plan carefully to avoid this. Most of the groundcover species will easily attain spreads of approximately 6 feet per mature plant.

Some of the best ones for groundcover are creeping cotoneaster (*C. adpressus*, Zones 4 to 8, slow growing, deciduous, 6 to 18 inches), bearberry cotoneaster (*C. dammeri*, Zones 5 to 8, fast growing, evergreen, to 1 foot), rock spray cotoneaster (*C. horizontalis*, Zones 4 to 7, fast growing, semievergreen, 2 to 3 feet) and willowleaf cotoneaster (*C. salicifolius* 'Repens', Zones 6 to 8, fast growing, evergreen to semievergreen, to 12 inches). Look for the variegated form of *C. horizontalis* to enliven an otherwise all-green planting.

Cultural Information: These are among the easiest of shrubs to grow, being flexible in their light requirements and seemingly indifferent about soil, too. They appreciate good drainage, however. Mass planting of cotoneaster may have a drawback: Like apples and pears, cotoneaster is susceptible to fire blight, a disease in which twigs may suddenly turn black or wither. Regularly observe plants and cut out any damaged wood and destroy it, sterilizing pruners between cuts with a dilute bleach solution.

Coyote brush; see *Baccharis*

Cotoneaster variegata

Creeper, winter; see *Euonymus*

Erica (EHR-ick-uh) heath, Moderate, evergreen ○ ◖

Zones: 5 to 9
Height: 1 foot
Flower Colors: White, pink, red
Characteristics: Like the heathers to which they are closely related, heaths are low-growing shrubby plants of a spreading habit. Their needlelike leaves are evergreen, and their flowers are produced over a period of several months. Spring heath (*E. carnea*) begins to perform in earliest spring; 'Ruby Glow' is a fine red, 'Winter Beauty' a deep pink tone. The Cornish heath (*E. vagans*) puts on its show July through October, 'Lyonesse' in white, 'Mrs. D. B. Maxwell' in pink or red. Heaths are fast growing and mix well with heathers and low-growing junipers. A rocky hillside sets them off handsomely.

Cultural Information: Heaths should be handled like heathers (see *Calluna*).

Euonymus (you-ON-ih-muss)
winter creeper, euonymus,
easy, evergreen. ○ ◐ ●
Zones: 4 to 9
Height: 4 to 12 inches, or grown as vine to 20 feet
Flower Color: Whitish
Characteristics: For the purpose of groundcover, the species _E. fortunei_ (sometimes called _E. radicans_) is the one to consider, and there is hardly an easier ev-

Euonymous fortunei _'Emerald Gaiety'_

Gaultheria procumbens

ergreen creeper or climber to be had. Because there are so many attractive foliage colors and forms to choose from, do not settle so quickly for just any old _Euonymus_. _E._ 'Colorata', for example, turns purple in winter; 'Emerald Gaiety' is a green-and-white variegate that adds a third color, pink, to the picture in the cold-weather months. _E. f._ 'Kewensis' is probably the daintiest of the lot, with its tiny green leaves marked with veins and its inclination to creep into a ground-hugging mat. The dark green leaves of shrubby 'Silver Queen' are edged in white. Don't be surprised if a single plant of _E. fortunei_ displays many different shapes and sizes of leaves; the tendency of winter creeper to sport, or mutate, is well known. Pinkish fruits are borne in fall on many varieties.

Cultural Information: Euonymous doesn't seem to care about light, soil moisture or much else—except when euonymus scale is present, and then nothing seems to go right. This tiny but highly destructive insect encrusts the plant parts with a whitish mess and may also produce yellow spots on the leaves. Cut out infested branches immediately and destroy. Sprays of horticultural oils have been shown to smother these soft-bodied insects, particularly if used promptly before an infestation gets more than a mere toehold. Oils can be sprayed on dormant plants and also those in leaf; follow the manufacturer's label directions carefully, and be certain to coat all plant parts, including undersides of leaves and stems; this may re-

quire taking those plants used as vines down from their supports.

Flowering blackberry; see
Rubus

Flowering raspberry; see
Rubus

Gaultheria procumbens
(gall-THEER-ee-uh pro-KUM-benz)
wintergreen, Easy, evergreen, native ◐ ●
Zones: 3 to 8
Height: 2 to 6 inches
Flower Color: White
Characteristics: Wintergreen is an acid-loving native shrub related to the blueberry, but producing bright red fruits instead. Not coincidentally, they have the flavor of wintergreen candies; oil of wintergreen is extracted from the fruit and foliage. Its small flowers are often obscured by the small, leathery leaves, but there is much else to recommend wintergreen. Its leaves take on a bronze-purple cast in cold weather, a stunning foil to the flashy berries in what is often an otherwise dull season on the forest floor. Wintergreen's home turf is the woodlands of eastern North America, and it will be at its best in such environments, where the light is filtered and the soil is peaty and moist. Use wintergreen in naturalistic plantings for best effect.

Cultural Information: Best to start with container-grown material, as wintergreen can be hard to transplant. When offered an acid soil that is full of organic material and thus moisture retentive, wintergreen can produce large mats of foliage and abundant berries.

Heath; see *Erica*

Heather; see *Calluna*

Hedera (HEAD-er-uh) **ivy,**
Easy, evergreen ○ ◑ ●
Zones: Varies, by species
Height: 6 to 8 inches, to 50
feet or more as a vine
Characteristics: Ivy is actually
a clinging vine, grabbing onto
its chosen support by means of
numerous rootlike structures
emerging from the main stem.
It is equally happy to grow over
the ground, and is commonly
used in masses under trees for
just that purpose. Unfortunately,
all too often gardeners choose
whatever anonymous dark-green
variety of English ivy (*Hedera
helix*) happens to be available
in flats at the local garden center and plant tray after tray of
the stuff, painting an unnecessarily dull picture. Take a hint
from the many showy variegates
available as house plants at the
florist or five-and-ten store: Ivy
needn't be plain. Besides intricate patterns of leaf color, including various greens with or
without splashes of white, cream
and yellow, some cultivars such
as *H. helix* 'Atropurpurea' take
on a bronze or purple cast in
winter. There are ivies with
leaves in sizes small to large,
some flat and others curled or
even frilly. More than a few
clever gardeners in our warmer
zones have purchased pots of
these "nonhardy" beauties and
dared to plant them outdoors,
to find that they fared just fine.
It's a matter of trial and error,
but the rewards may be worth it
if even a single kind survives.
Better yet, scour nurseries and
catalogs for better-looking stock

of the proven-to-be-hardy stuff,
such as the cultivars *H. h.*
'Aureo-variegata' (green and yellow) or *H. h.* 'Argenteo-variegata'
(green and white). In the coldest limits of its hardiness, ask
for *H. h.* 'Baltic' or 'Bulgaria';
H. h. 'Wilsonii' is rated to Zone
4, probably the toughest *H. helix*
in cultivation.

Although neither on its own
is particularly exciting, pachysandra and ivy mixed helps
the appearance of both; when
this blend is underplanted with
small spring bulbs, it is of even
greater interest. Ivy interplanted
with bloodroot (*Sanguinaria
canadensis*) would be even nicer.

Ivies are great for out-of-the-
way places you don't want to
deal with, as they tend to be
largely carefree, a fine lawn substitute on hilly banks, for ex-

Hedera canariensis *'Variegata'*

ample, that would be difficult
or impossible to mow.

H. helix, if it gets a chance
to climb, ages in a way that
may surprise a gardener who
has not been forewarned and will

Hedera helix *'Glacier'*

likely think that something is wrong. When a climbing plant is about to reach flowering and fruiting age (the flowers are small and whitish, the berries usually black) it becomes positively shrublike in spots, producing more upright stems covered with leaves that don't look like ivy at all. Instead of the characteristic lobed leaves, the adult ones are oval and lobeless. Upright vines of some age get quite woody, and can even be destructive to facades, windows and eaves.

mixed Helianthemum *species*

Hypericum *species*

Less hardy (Zones 8 to 10), but boasting wine-colored twigs and leaf stalks (petioles), is Algerian ivy (*H. canariensis*), a popular groundcover in California. Its large leaves are shiny; the variegated forms are particularly attractive. Persian ivy (*H. colchica*, Zones 6 to 9) has large leaves too, but they are not lobed. The cultivar *H. colchica* 'Sulphur Heart' has leaves mottled with yellow and light green; it would quickly brighten a planting of plain green *H. Helix*. *Cultural Information:* Well-drained soil is to ivy's liking, and it is best if the planting area is well prepared so that the soil is also of an organic nature. Particularly in the first year, ivy must be kept watered to become established; after that, it will be less demanding of watering provided the soil was well prepared, and it will also grow much faster. For shady exposures, the dark green leaf forms are the best bet, though these can also tolerate some sun; variegates with yellow and white zones need more light, and are also usually somewhat more tender. Many ivies suffer winter damage from extremes of cold and dryness; do not hesitate to prune in early spring, which not only will remove unsightly portions but will also promote lusher, more compact growth. When planting ivy on a wall or trellis, take future painting needs into account, because a mature display of it is no small matter to take down. Ivy will gladly make a chain-link fence or other undesirable vertical vista disappear. Propagate by cuttings, rooted in moist sand.

Helianthemum (hee-lee-AN-them-um) sunrose, Easy, evergreen to semievergreen ○

Zones: 5 or 6 to 10
Height: 6 to 12 inches
Flower Colors: White, yellow, orange, pink, red
Characteristics: The sunroses are shrubs of a trailing habit that cover themselves in roselike flowers over a long period from late spring into summer. Rebloom is also possible. *H. nummularium*, the most common garden species, is an undemanding plant, happy to grow in poor, dry soil like that of its native Mediterranean region. It is a good choice for rock gardens and many seaside locales. 'Fireball' is a low, double red; 'St. Mary's' has large white blooms. *Cultural Information:* In sunny spots with sharp drainage, sunroses won't ask much of you. Pruning after the first major flower show fades will promote a late-season rebloom; plants in cooler zones can be cut back partway in earliest spring to remove any winter damage and promote denser growth.

Hypericum (hy-PER-ick-um) St.-John's-wort, Easy, evergreen to deciduous ○ ◑

Zones: 6 to 9
Height: most 1 to 3 feet
Flower Color: Yellow
Characteristics: Hypericum is a diverse genus, comprising plants that are herbaceous, semiwoody and woody, too. The best of the lot for the purpose of covering the ground is the Aaron's-beard St.-John's-wort (*H. calycinum*), a shrubby type that enthusiastically roots along the ground regularly wherever its sprawling branches touch moist earth. It

is semievergreen or evergreen, about 1 foot high, with big, bright yellow flowers that keep coming from midsummer to frost. Tolerates dry soils and even sandy ones.

Cultural Information: H. calycinum is a toughie that asks little of the gardener, but a hard pruning when it gets out of hand or its performance begins to fade is much appreciated. Easily divided.

Iberis (eye-BEER-iss) **perennial candytuft,** Easy, evergreen to semievergreen ○

Zones: 4 to 9
Height: 6 to 12 inches
Flower Color: White
Characteristics: Iberis sempervirens, the subshrub known as perennial candytuft, covers itself in white flowers from spring into summer. The cultivar *I. s.* 'Snowflake' is highly recommended for its larger, dense flower heads; it reblooms later in the season with more regularity than others. Candytuft is a mainstay of many rock gardens and is happiest in sunny, fast-draining spots. Its clear white cloud is also handsome as a foil for tulips and other bright-colored spring bulbs.

Cultural Information: Average garden soil is best for perennial candytuft. Cut back hard after flowering, by about halfway or more, to keep it in good form. It may also rebloom if handled this way. Propagate by cuttings in summer.

Ivy; see *Hedera*

Japanese spurge; see *Pachysandra*

Juniper; see *Juniperus*

Juniperus (joo-NIP-er-us) **juniper,** Easy, evergreen ○

Zones: varies by species
Height: 6 inches and up
Characteristics: Junipers have much to recommend them, not the least of which is durability virtually unmatched by any other evergreen. Their foliage is frequently steely blue or silvery gray in color, though some varieties are sold as being turquoise (*J. horizontalis* 'Turquoise Spreader', for example), or yellow (*J. h.* 'Pfitzerana Aurea'), and others for the tendency to take on a plum-colored cast in cold weather (*J. h.* 'Plumosa', for instance). Variegated junipers are also available. There are so many cultivars that one needs a directory to keep them straight; most are great improvements over the earliest one, 'Pfitzerana', which is simply too wide at maturity (10 or more feet) for most applications. They are tolerant of a wide range of soils, although in general they are at their best in somewhat moist, light ones. Some exceptions: For sandy soil, try shore juniper (*J. conferta*, Zones 6 to 9), including the varieties 'Blue Pacific' and 'Emerald Sea', or *J. horizontalis* (Zones 3 to 9), a very wide-spreading species that includes the famed cultivars 'Bar Harbor' and 'Blue Chip'. All of these are about 1 foot high. The lowest-growing juniper is another *J. horizontalis*, namely 'Wiltonii' or 'Blue Rug', whose needles are intensely silver-blue changing to pale plum in the cold.

In addition to their general sturdiness, junipers can withstand heavy pruning, too, but

Iberis sempervirens, *lower right*

this is not an excuse for planting them too closely in the first place, then butchering them into submission. Many popular groundcover junipers are robust spreaders, so give them room. One thing junipers won't tolerate well is lack of sunshine, so don't install a planting in the shade; it will soon become ratty.

Cultural Information: Grow junipers in sun, in well-drained soil. They are susceptible to a fungal twig blight that has been named specifically for them, *Phomopsis juniperovora*. Particularly in nursery situations, or when overplanted in the landscape, this can prove very costly. *J. horizontalis* and *J. procumbens* are among the worst hit of the clan. Determine that the plants you purchase are blight-resistant

Juniperus horizontalis 'Venusta'

ones in the first place, as prevention is easier than cure.

Lilac, wild; see *Ceanothus*

Manzanita; see *Arctostaphylos*

Mitchella repens

Pachysandra procumbens

Mitchella repens (mich-ELL-uh rep-pens) **partridgeberry,** Moderate, evergreen, native ◑
Zones: 3 to 9
Height: 1 to 4 inches
Flower Color: White
Characteristics: Partridgeberry is more frequently seen as a delicate-textured Christmas green in holiday arrangements than it is in the wild, but it is more at home on the floor of its native northeastern woodlands. Small spring flowers are followed in late summer or fall by bright red fruits (white in the case of the variety *M. r. leucocarpa*); the tiny evergreen leaves are marked with pale veins.
Cultural Information: A woodland native, partridgeberry likes acid, somewhat moist soil. The addition of ample amounts of peat humus would be appropriate for a place you'd like to grow *Mitchella.* This is not a plant that will cooperate in hot, sunny exposures. Propagate by layering (see *Calluna* for this technique).

Myrtle; see *Vinca*

Pachysandra (pack-iss-AND-ruh) **Japanese spurge, Alleghany spurge,** Easy, evergreen or deciduous, one native ◑ ●
Zones: 4 to 9
Height: 6 to 12 inches
Flower Color: White
Characteristics: A plant that will thrive even in dry shade—the bane of many—is a friend indeed. *Pachysandra terminalis,* Japanese spurge, is such a plant, and hence it is one of the most-used groundcovers in the gardening repertory, particularly up north. Sometimes, though, too much of a good thing can simply be too much. "A sea of plastic-looking army green" is how one gardening friend describes the plain green form that is often overplanted. Avoid the same mistake and break up the monotony by introducing an island of the white-marked form *P. t.* 'Variegata' within the mass, or interweave splashes of a showy ivy (*Hedera* species) into it. Underplant *Pachysandra* with spring bulbs, whose fading foliage will be well hidden in its thick, leafy cover. Good news: Improved green versions are being introduced featuring more interesting leaf forms (serrated edges, oak-leaf–shaped leaves, and smaller ones, too) and finishes. *P. terminalis* is evergreen. Lamentably too few garden-

ers know the botanical cousin of *P. terminalis*, *P. procumbens*, which is actually the native member of the genus; Alleghany spurge is its common name. Reliably evergreen in the South, where it comes from, and behaving like a herbaceous plant in the North, it grows into handsome, naturally rounded clumps. It is outstanding at the base of trees in woodland settings, or used in juxtaposition to the Japanese form.

Cultural Information: P. terminalis is susceptible to euonymous scale, which can be disastrous (see *Euonymous*). Generally speaking, however, this is a trouble-free plant you can rely on. Don't hesitate to give *Pachysandra* a haircut if the planting looks shabby; while you're at it, you can propagate more plants. Increase Japanese spurge by cuttings in early summer, or by division; Alleghany spurge should be divided just as the growing season begins in early spring.

Partridgeberry; see **Mitchella**

Perennial candytuft; see **Iberis**

Periwinkle; see **Vinca**

Potentilla (po-ten-TILL-uh) **cinquefoil**, Easy, deciduous or evergreen, some natives ○
Zones: 3 to 8
Height: 2 inches to 6 feet
Flower Colors: Shades of orange, red, pink, white, yellow
Characteristics: The genus *Potentilla* is diverse, with more

than 500 species, including woody plants and herbaceous perennials alike. Some generalizations can be made: The cinquefoils are durable, basically disease and pest resistant and, more often than not, free-flowering over a long period. The smaller forms of shrubby *P. fruticosa* make a good intermediate-height groundcover of approximately 2 feet; look for 'Abbotswood' (white flowers, just over 24 inches) or 'Yellow Gem' (yellow, about 18 inches). They will bloom from late spring through late summer and are deciduous.

P. verna (or *P. tabernaemontanii*) is a creeping form just several inches high; its flowers are butter colored. *P. cinerea*, around the same height, also has yellow blooms. Both are evergreen. *P. nitida* forms dense mats just an inch or two high and flowers in pinkish tones in late spring or early summer. It is slightly less cold hardy, to about Zone 5.

Cultural Information: The cinquefoils want sunny exposures and sharp drainage for peak performance, although in hottest zones some relief from midday sun is appreciated as it tends to wash out flowers of darker hue. They do not ask for lots of water, either; these are tough plants. With *P. fruticosa*, shrubs may get scraggly after a few years and will benefit from having the oldest stems removed; they can take a harder overall pruning if it seems warranted. Increase cinquefoils by softwood cuttings in summer.

Raspberry, flowering; see **Rubus**

Potentilla '*Gold Drop*'

Rosmarinus (rose-ma-RYE-nus) **rosemary**, Easy, evergreen ○ ◆
Zones: Various
Height: 1 to 4 feet or more
Flower Colors: Lavender, white
Characteristics: One of the sorrows of gardening in Zone 5, or

Rosmarinus *species*

even on the border of 6 and 7 (as I did not so long ago), is the necessity of treating rosemary as a tender perennial, hauling it indoors each winter. Next to lavender, another finicky creature when it comes to –20° winters, rosemary is my favorite scent. This nose would gladly forsake every last rose, and maybe even peonies and lilacs, for one whiff of its aromatic needlelike foliage. Imagine my jealousy at learning that in northern California, for instance, the prostrate form of this delightful plant carpets the medians of shopping centers and whole hillsides, blooming in winter or spring. Low-growing *R. officinalis* 'Prostratus' is a handsome groundcover; hardy in Zones 8

Rubus calycinoides

to 10, it is the most tender rosemary of all. It may grow as high as 2 feet, but can be trimmed shorter; the closely related 'Huntington Carpet' is lower, about 18 inches at the most. The more familiar, shrubby form common to the herb garden, *R. officinalis* (hardy to Zone 6 if protected), with a gray-green cast to the foliage, can withstand shearing and thereby be kept around 2 feet tall. It blooms in early summer.
Cultural Information: Rosemary is a sun-loving plant requiring good drainage; it is also quite drought tolerant and hardly fussy about soil. Keep rosemary from the drying effects of windy wintertime sites. When winter damage occurs, wait until early spring after frost danger is past and then trim back tips until live (green) wood is revealed. Increase by cuttings or layering (see *Calluna*).

Rosemary; see **Rosmarinus**

Rubus (ROO-bus) **bramble, flowering blackberry, flowering raspberry,** Easy, evergreen ○ ◑
Zones: 7 to 9
Height: 6 to 12 inches
Flower Color: White
Characteristics: The first time I saw *Rubus calycinoides*, the flowering blackberry (it has flowers, but no fruit, hence the common name), I admired its leaf shape, which is slightly reminiscent of that of the geranium, and its robust habit of growth. The next time I saw it, I was completely hooked. It was in fall, and the leaves had taken

on a brilliant red mottling in contrast to their basic fuzzy, deeply textured green. The foliage looks as if it's covered with white felt on its undersides. I am told that *R. calycinoides* is a bit aggressive for use in certain spots, but when what you want is to cover the ground, that zeal will suit just fine. This blackberry is thornless, by the way.
Cultural Information: Well-drained soil is the preference of *R. calycinoides*, which has only recently appeared in catalogs and at nurseries with any regularity. Its hardiness is rated only as cold as Zone 7, but I am inclined to try it a bit farther north, because it looks anything but delicate. Increase by division, or by layering (see *Calluna*).

Spurge, Alleghany; see **Pachysandra**

Spurge, Japanese; see **Pachysandra**

St.-John's-wort; see **Hypericum**

Sunrose; see **Helianthemum**

Vinca (VIN-ka) **periwinkle, myrtle,** Easy, evergreen ◑ ○
Zones: Vary
Height: 6 to 24 inches
Flower Colors: White, blue, wine, lavender

Characteristics: Vinca, along with *Pachysandra* and ivy, rates as one of the "big three" of groundcovers. It has a finer texture than the others plus the asset of phloxlike flowers that are long lasting in spring. I am fortunate that a nearby nursery appreciates not just the energetic, durable qualities of plain old *Vinca minor* (Zones 4 to 10), but also the far more satisfying aesthetic of its best varieties. The nursery's selection includes variegated-leaf forms (white-edged 'Sterling Silver' and yellow-veined 'Aureola', both with blue flowers), a wine-flowered one that would be smashing with daffodils and a dainty white ('Miss Jekyll') that is easier on the eyes and in plant combinations than some of the more common periwinkle blue ones. A double-flowered form is harder to come by, but one can keep hoping to happen on it someday.

Vinca minor and *Vinca major* (larger-leaved, hardy Zones 7 to 10 or slightly colder with protection or in a mild-winter year) are really vines, with no capacity to climb. Instead, they trail along the ground or would happily cascade from containers or window boxes. In the North, the larger form is popular and sold as an annual for just that purpose. *V. major* comes in a cream-and-green leaf form, labeled 'Variegata' or 'Elegantissima', with blue flowers.

Vinca minor makes an excellent underplanting for shrubs and trees; don't forget to tuck some springtime bulbs into it for additional interest. *Vinca* is also appropriate for hillsides and other sloping terrain.

Cultural Information: Vinca is extremely flexible about light and will grow in any reasonably decent soil. To promote thicker growth, or to clean up from damage, mow or shear at a high height. Cuttings (semihardened, in summer) can be used to propagate new plants, or divide to increase.

Vinca minor

Vines

Like most average home landscapes, my own garden is short on architectural features. The grand gardens of English picture books may have them, but at my place, no stone lions guard the driveway, nor is there a fountain to form a focal point in my backyard.

Bring on the vines, I say, as it is with the plants that climb that even such a modest scene acquires a sense of architecture fast. But too often overlooked is the ability of many vines to grow horizontally, too, either on their own or woven through an otherwise uninspiring evergreen groundcover, for instance. Three of the best vines for thick, evergreen cover on the ground, *Euonymus*, *Vinca* and *Hedera*, are detailed in their own individual entries.

The real workhorses of enduring three-dimension landscapes are perennial and woody vines, but there are good an-

Parthenocissus quinquefolia

Clematis *'Nelly Moser'*

Wisteria and climbing 'Lady Banks' rose

nual choices suited to a quick-fix or splash of vertical color while you wait for that *Clematis* to get up the trellis. Canarybird vine (*Tropaeolum peregrinum*) is one zesty candidate, or try cup-and-saucer vine (*Cobaea scandens*), hyacinth bean (*Dolichos lablab*) or variegated Japanese hops (*Humulus japonicus variegatus*), to cite some showy examples.

On to the perennials: A porch shaded by Dutchman's pipe vine (*Aristolochia durior*, Zones 4 to 8) could not be cooler, its leaves are so dense. Give this vigorous twiner lots of elbow room. Even the horror of a chain-link fence can look positively romantic when sweet autumn clematis (*Clematis paniculata*, hardy to Zone 5) clambers over it, cloaking its harsh reality with an effusion of foliage and sweet-scented flowers. The most modest of walls will be ablaze in color come fall when Boston ivy (*Parthenocissus tricuspidata*, Zones 4 to 8) climbs it. (Exercise caution when growing strong woody vines like the ivies up wooden shingles, which may be dislodged, and also keep in mind that they will leave a hard-to-clean residue behind on wood and other surfaces. Trim back well clear of windows, which may be damaged by insistent vines.)

For fragrance, there are many choices, including the honeysuckles, wisteria and jasmines. The flowers of members of the genus *Passiflora* are wildly exotic, and they offer green-to-yellow fruit, too. For leaf color, the hardy kiwi (*Actinidia kolomikta*) has green leaves splashed with pink and white (Zone 5). The variegated porcelain berry (*Ampelopsis brevipedunculata* 'Elegans') is showy, too; areas of pink-red and white decorate the current growth.

An intertwining of climbing hydrangea (*Hydrangea anomala petiolaris*, Zones 4 to 7), and the Japanese hydrangea vine (*Schizophragma hydrangeoides*) will give a longer season of bloom to the planting. Likewise, a climbing rose mingling with a late-blooming clematis translates to color most of the summer.

Two jasmines appropriate for landscape use, the yellow-flowered *Jasminum nudiflorum* (Zones 6 to 10) and the less-hardy pink-flowered *J. polyanthum* (Zones 9 to 10), are deliciously scented. So are many of the honeysuckles; a favorite for its long season of bloom and gaudy pink and yellow flowers is *Lonicera heckrottii* (Zones 4 to 9), the goldflame honeysuckle.

Exercise caution with such rampant growers as *Wisteria* species (Zones 4 to 9) and the trumpet vine (*Campsis radicans*, Zones 4 to 9) and also with fast-growing silver fleece vine (*Polygonum aubertii*, Zones 4 to 7), which quickly forms a cloud of white late-summer flowers. They can be beautiful additions to the landscape if kept in bounds by the gardener. The green form of porcelain berry (*Ampelopsis*) and certain honeysuckles, notably Hall's, are serious weeds in many areas of the country, however. It is probably best to avoid planting them; this goes for the robust bittersweet (*Celastrus* species), too, because this weedy creature is strangling more-desirable trees and shrubs throughout the American landscape.

Wild lilac; see ***Ceanothus***

Winter creeper; see ***Euonymus***

Wintergreen; see ***Gaultheria***

PESTS AND DISEASES

WITH A LITTLE HELP FROM MY FRIENDS

In the more than five years that I have been working it, my current garden has never suffered a serious infestation of pest or disease. Sure, there have been losses—usually to fits of extreme weather like a swampy spring followed by a droughtlike summer, or a winter with no protective snow cover in sight.

I cannot take all the credit for my good fortune, however. I suspect it is mostly the work of the extraordinarily large population of birds, snakes and toads I share the place with, and I thank them. Come to think of it, they are probably thanking me for leaving the place a little bit wild here and there, just the way they like it.

Too many home gardens have no such creatures, or only messy, pesky birds like pigeons or shockingly successful opportunists like cowbirds—parasites who actually dare to lay their eggs in other birds' nests. Urbanization and suburbanization of the nation has eliminated much of the good creatures' former habitats and also forced large garden nuisances, like deer, into closer proximity with humans.

The bulldozer has certainly left its mark, but that doesn't prevent gardeners from cultivating the kind of habitat, in miniature, that will lure these helpful allies back. Even the tiniest effort—installing a bird bath, a feeder or two, letting a brush pile remain year 'round in some out-of-the-way corner—will quickly increase wildlife activity in even the most dire and seemingly inhospitable of circumstances. Did you ever witness the excitement a single mud puddle could generate in not just birds, but also the spice-bush swallowtail butterfly? I have seen migrating songbirds stop to rest a while at the roof garden on one of the skyscrapers in New York City's Rockefeller Center complex; in a densely populated area of suburban Long Island, an organic-gardening friend attracts species of birds that even his immediate neighbors haven't seen in years.

On the subject of organic gardening: Stopping the use of toxic poisons—fertilizers, pesticides, herbicides and fungicides of chemical formulation—will help most of all in your efforts to rebuild a semblance of a habitat. Tiny creatures like reptiles, amphibians, birds and insects are highly sensitive to these materials and simply cannot survive around them in many cases. Stop using lawn chemicals and your earthworm population will magically rebound, too. A gardener has no better friend in the work of soil building than these amazing humus producers; don't kill them off for the vanity of a picture-perfect, weed-free lawn.

PREVENTION: EASIER THAN CURE

When I do come up against trouble of any kind, I adhere to the basic principles of IPM, integrated pest management. Although it is not strictly an organic approach, IPM is the most sensible philosophy available to help farmers, gardeners and even apartment dwellers besieged by cockroaches or homeowners tested by termites in the basement or moths in their sweater drawer to fight back. It shows them how to do so without unnecessary negative environmental impact—in other words, in the least toxic way possible.

IPM is a step-by-step process of prevention, regular monitoring and quick treatment that combines to reduce chemical use dramatically. IPM allows for the use of chemicals as a last resort, once all other, safer options have been exhausted, and then only in a pinpoint manner, right on the spot that is affected. In IPM, you don't spray for gypsy moth annually because you fear it might appear; you monitor the signs of a potential outbreak, then weigh the evidence before deciding whether to treat. (In my own garden, if I get to the point at which chemicals are the only way out, I opt to lose the plant; gardeners who wish to be strictly organic, as I do, will have to face this eventuality every so often.)

IPM is not just a way of treating problems; it is a sound way to garden. It stresses that proper cultural practices—how you water, mulch, feed, prune, clean up and even plant in the first place—influence how disease and pest resistant your garden will be. Practices that should seem obvious are all too often overlooked by gardeners who prefer to buy a can of chemical spray and tackle the mess after the fact. Growing a sun-loving plant in the shade may not kill it immediately, but if an outbreak of pests or disease strikes, how well will the sluggish, stunted creature fare against it? A well-grown plant would stand a chance, particularly if detection and treatment were made early. Why not follow proper cultural recommendations in the first place, instead of waging a losing battle and then trying a quick fix with chemicals?

More and more, as environmental consciousness deepens, information on IPM practices appropriate for plants grown in your region is being distributed by local botanical gardens and cooperative extension services. Research breakthroughs in safe control methods—beneficial parasites that attack a specific pest, for instance, or environmentally sensitive "germ warfare" tactics—are being made all the time, so IPM recommendations are updated frequently. Ask for them; the institutions usually offer this information in flyer or pamphlet form for a small charge or even free, as part of their consumer-education efforts.

STEPS TO A HEALTHY GARDEN

1. Prepare your soil well (for details, see Chapter 3). Healthy soil means healthy plants. Don't skimp.
2. Don't fight the site. Woodland shade-lovers don't want to grow on a sun-baked cliff by the seashore; plants of Mediterranean origin probably aren't desirous of a home in a marshland. Pay attention to a plant's needs; learn where it came from and what it wants to be happy. Move plants that look peaked to another site; then, if they still falter, throw them out or give them away to someone who can provide a more appropriate environment.
3. Practice good housekeeping. Clean up spent plants and debris as it accumulates, except when it has ornamental value, as in the case of striking dried seedheads.
4. Replenish mulches as needed to preserve soil moisture, thwart weeds and prevent soil compaction. Don't mulch too deeply, though—never more than a couple of inches. You will otherwise risk smothering plants, depriving them of water completely, and creating ideal hiding places for certain pests.
5. Water carefully, neither in the heat of midday nor in the dark of night. The former wastes water to evaporation and can also cause plants undue stress; the latter encourages those demons of the darkness, slugs and snails.

MEET THE ENEMY

Nowhere is there a garden without a chewed leaf or two. Expecting perfection would be useless, and such unrealistic expectations are what led to excessive chemical usage in the first place. A degree of trouble is likely to befall even the most conscientious gardener. Most of the plants recommended in this book are relatively trouble free, which is why they are good choices even for large-scale uses as groundcovers. In certain cases where a particular disease or pest is common to a plant, this was noted in the individual plant portrait, along with a suggested control method. Some of the most common opponents you are likely to face follow.

APHIDS: These small, soft-bodied sucking insects sap a plant's vigor and also spread disease as they work. Aphids are nothing to panic about, though, except in the most extreme of circumstances. Usually a stiff spray of water from the hose will knock them off and drown them. Or use an insecticidal soap solution, such as the one manufactured by Safer's, according to package directions.

Aphids

BEETLES: Beetles, as everyone who has seen one knows, are hungry, hard-bodied chewing insects. Japanese beetles are a scourge of gardeners east of the Mississippi. They can be hand picked (drown or crush them) if you are diligent. Some gardeners use traps baited with pheromone lures, which fool the beetles into thinking a prospective mate is nearby, but recently the use of such traps has been questioned as it may actually attract more beetles than you would otherwise have in the garden. Ask your local extension service for up-to-the-minute advice.

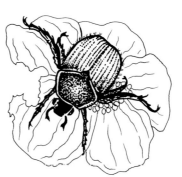

Beetle

Japanese beetle

DEER: I have lost more plants to deer than to any other pest since I began gardening in the country. I have tried various traditional deterrents, including hanging aluminum pie plates in the trees to scare them off, applying foul-smelling substances like blood meal and solutions made from putrefied eggs, and so forth. From my experience, I would say that deer and gardens do not mix; don't fight that basic fact. Get a fence, and make it electric, if possible. Local landscape services, nurseries or the extension service in your area know the most effective fencing systems for deer; seek professional advice before making the investment.

MOLES: Contrary to common misconception, moles are not rodents at all. They do not generally eat plant parts; they are insectivorous, feasting on worms and grubs primarily, but in the process of tunneling through lawn and garden they make a horrible mess. Moles are solitary creatures and slow to reproduce, so it is unusual for more than one or two adults to live in a single acre of land. Trapping is the only effective control; don't try poison bait (remember, they eat bugs, not nuts or seeds).

RABBITS AND WOOD-CHUCKS: Unless you are inclined to trap these large rodents, you may face wholesale destruction of the garden. Fencing is effective, if it is installed underground, too, to thwart burrowing, and if the gauge of the fencing material is small enough so animals cannot pass through.

SNAILS AND SLUGS: These soft-bodied creatures are very sensitive to the surface they slither over, so the application of a barrier of rough-textured diatomaceous earth (an organic material available as a powder at the garden center) will deter them. Sunken saucers or cleaned cat-food cans of beer will lure these night feeders in for a drunken swim before they drown. Gardeners with strong stomachs should venture out into the night with a flashlight and a can of very salty water and drown them in it.

Leaves damaged by the following pests, from left: beetles, flea beetles, caterpillars, aphids and leafhoppers.

Slug

Snail

Caterpillars are Butterflies-to-be

As contrary as it may sound to pest-phobic gardeners, to grow a true butterfly garden you must lure caterpillars into your landscape, too. That's the message from the National Wildlife Federation and other experts, who warn that providing only colorful flowers for adult butterflies falls short of creating an ideal habitat. Butterflies' principal diet is the flower nectar; plant colorful flowers en masse in sunny spots for best results. But in its larval stage—when it is a caterpillar—the butterfly-to-be needs food, shelter and water, too.

Caterpillars are leaf eaters. And some, like the American painted lady caterpillar, are fussy leaf eaters. Two groundcover plants do please its palate, though: pussytoes (Antennaria, a fuzzy gray groundcover for well-drained, acidic soil), and pearly everlasting (Anaphalis). The yellow, black-and-white larval form of the monarch butterfly is picky, too: It feeds only on milkweeds (Asclepias species). Some other recommendations: Grow red clover or alfalfa for sulfur butterfly larvae; parsley, dill, lovage or fennel for the swallowtails; milkweeds for monarchs and queens.

GARDENERS' MOST-ASKED QUESTIONS

Q: What are some groundcovers for part shade?
A: *Aegopodium, Asarum, Chrysogonum, Convallaria, Epimedium,* ferns, *Galax, Galium, Hedera, Helleborus, Hosta, Houttuynia, Lamiastrum, Lamium, Pachysandra, Pulmonaria, Tiarella* and *Vinca* are among the shade-tolerant groundcovers.

Q: Which groundcovers can be used for erosion control on a slope or hillside?
A: *Arctostaphylos, Baccharis, Ceanothus, Cotoneaster, Hypericum, Juniperus* and *Rosa* species are among the best shrubby choices for covering on a slope. The low-growing rosemary, and several other herbs such as lavender and santolina, are possibilities, too. A mixed planting of heaths and heathers, perhaps with the addition of prostrate junipers, or a low-growing bamboo might suit your purpose as well.

Q: My soil is quite acidic; are there some groundcovers that like acid soil?
A: Woodland plants, which grow in at least part shade, tend to hail from acidic soils. Some groundcovers of that type include bunchberry (*Cornus canadensis*), bloodroot (*Sanguinaria canadensis*), *Galax*, various ferns, wintergreen (*Gaultheria procumbens*), wild ginger and *Asarum*. In sunnier positions, try bearberry or manzanita (*Arctostaphylos* species), *Paxistima*, potentilla and heaths and heathers.

Q: I want to be more careful with water, but how can I grow a lawn without it?
A: In the case of most traditional lawn grasses and grass mixes, particularly in warmer zones or summertime conditions, you can't grow a lawn without supplemental moisture.

Removing and replanting your lawn with a more drought-resistant grass such as one of the tall fescues is a possibility to consider; changing portions of the lawn to alternative plantings, such as an herb garden, shrub border or masses of other drought-tolerant groundcovers, is another.

Meanwhile, though, water wisely in the following ways: Dethatch regularly (by vigorous raking out of dead material, or

Burpee employees hard at work in the shipping department in 1910.

use a special dethatcher that can be rented), so every drop can penetrate. Water early in the day, not during the heat of midday when evaporation will waste much of the water. Reduce fertilizer usage, as forcing lots of green growth means more water will be needed to support it.

Q: *What are some gray-leaved groundcovers?*
A: *Anaphalis, Antennaria, Artemisia* and *Stachys* are some of the best gray groundcovers.

Q: *What are some groundcovers with golden foliage?*
A: Try the yellow-leaved ivies, hostas, golden sage, moneywort (*Lysimachia nummularia*) and feverfew.

Q: *What do I do about poison ivy? It's creeping into a bed of pachysandra, and under and up several trees in my yard.*
A: Chemicals, of course, have been the traditional means of eradicating poison ivy (*Toxicodendron radicans*). I do not recommend using them. When handled carefully, poison ivy can be kept in check much more safely, from an environmental standpoint, by simply pruning it back so hard several seasons in a row that it cannot survive.

Wearing a long-sleeved shirt, trousers, boots with pant legs tucked into them and gloves (I like to use disposable surgical gloves or washable ones for this task), I start to fight the ivy as early in the season as possible, preferably before it is fully leafed out. This is not because I wish to avoid the allergy-causing leaves; every part of the ivy plant, dormant or active, roots and all, can stimulate a rash in allergic individuals, so beware. But it is easier to maneuver around semidormant plants than those that are in full leaf, and after pruning, there is less waste to dispose of.

Cut out every bit of the plant with a hand pruner (a saw may be required if the specimen at hand is a major woody vine), making lowest cuts near soil level. Clean all tools and bag up cuttings before removing your protective gear. Never burn any part of poison ivy (inhaled in smoke form, ivy toxins can cause highly dangerous pulmonary rashes), and don't compost it. Discard with the trash. Repeat as new vines emerge later in the season and thereafter; eventually the lack of leaves, meaning no photosynthesis, will kill the plants.

In recent years, a liquid skin cleanser called Tecnu has been promoted to wash away any residual toxic oils, and there are barrier creams to apply beforehand to keep the oils off the skin in the first place, too. You may wish to try one or both products if you are particularly sensitive.

If you do resort to chemical forms of removal, please follow this advice: Always select the least-toxic product that will satisfactorily perform the job. Overkill, besides being unnecessary, can be lethal to individual and environment.

Q: *Which groundcovers can withstand poor, dry soil conditions?*
A: Among the groundcovers that can stand lean, dry soil are *Agave, Anaphalis, Antennaria, Arabis, Arctostaphylos* species, *Baccharis, Cerastium, Cotoneaster, Hypericum*, ice plants, *Opuntia, Phlox subulata*, and some *Sedum*. Many herbs, including *Santolina* and prostrate rosemary, will also fare well in such spots.

Q: *I want to do something about weeds under the shrubs lining my driveway, mostly hollies, azaleas and yew.*
A: Groundcovers form a living mulch that helps to hold back weeds. Ivy, *Pachysandra* and *Vinca* are frequently used for this purpose, but there are other possibilities. A fast-growing groundcover like yellow archangel (*Lamiastrum galeobdolon*) will fill in quickly and be mostly evergreen. The lamiums, particularly *Lamium maculatum* 'White Nancy' and 'Beacon Silver', have outstanding foliage patterns and give good cover spring through fall. The multicolored bugleweeds (*Ajuga reptans*) are semievergreen and paint an appealing mosaic on the ground. Low-growing astilbes like *Astilbe chinensis pumila* offer groundcoverage as well as flowers, as do hostas.

Q: *Are there any deer-proof groundcovers?*
A: Generally speaking, deer will eat almost anything when hungry, even some plants said to be poisonous or otherwise unappealing. Thorny plants like *Berberis* and pungent-smelling or aromatic ones like the herbs *Santolina, Rosmarinus* and *Lavandula* are also less attractive than many others. Plants with thick, felted leaves like *Stachys*

seem to be of little interest to deer and rabbits, who appear to share somewhat similar tastes.

Q: I love my clematis vine, but I am at a loss as to how to prune it and otherwise care for it properly.

A: What clematis want most of all is a good planting hole: well-prepared soil at least 2 feet deep and 2 feet across, enhanced with peat, sand and a handful of lime. Feed established plants twice a year with a 5-10-10 fertilizer, preferably one of an all-natural organic formula.

Early-blooming clematis don't require pruning becuase they bloom on last year's wood; cutting them back will reduce the wood that can bear flowers. Summer-flowering clematis bloom on new growth, so prune hard, to about 6 to 12 inches from the base, in early spring. Those that bloom on old and new wood give you an option: For early, large flowers, don't prune. For medium flowers later on, prune hard.

Q: I am interested in growing native plants. Which groundcovers should I use?

A: Native plants for groundcover include *Asarum*, bunchberry (*Cornus canadensis*), *Ceanothus*, *Chrysogonum*, *Galax*, *Gaultheria*, *Heuchera*, *Paxistima canbyi*, *Phlox*, *Sanguinaria*, *Shortia*, *Tiarella*, *Vancouveria* and *Waldsteinia*, plus numerous ferns and some grasses.

Q: Flooding submerged part of my lawn and garden in salt water. Can they be saved?

A: Any sustained submersion in salt water will kill most garden plants, including turf grass. Immediate fresh-water irrigation of the affected soil areas is essential if plants are to stand a chance. Repeat frequently to leach harmful salts.

Applying gypsum (calcium sulfate), 50 pounds per 1,000 square feet of soil surface, and watering it in well speeds the leaching out of salt. Do not plant anything until the soil tests clean; have it evaluated by your local cooperative extension or private laboratory.

Q: I have heard that zoysia grass uses less water and fertilizer than other lawn grasses. Is it true?

A: Many people have heard extravagant advertising claims about a "miracle" lawn. Zoysia is indeed a quick-growing, cushiony turf for sun that can withstand high heat, somewhat poorer soil and closer mowing than many lawn grasses. It can thrive with less water and fertilizer, too. But zoysia will be tan, not green, from around October to May in cool-weather zones. It is also not entirely disease and pest resistant, subject to such troubles as grubs, chinch bugs and rust.

Please write or call for a free Burpee catalog:

W. Atlee Burpee & Company
300 Park Avenue
Warminster, PA 18974
215-674-9633

Appendix

THE USDA PLANT HARDINESS MAP OF THE UNITED STATES

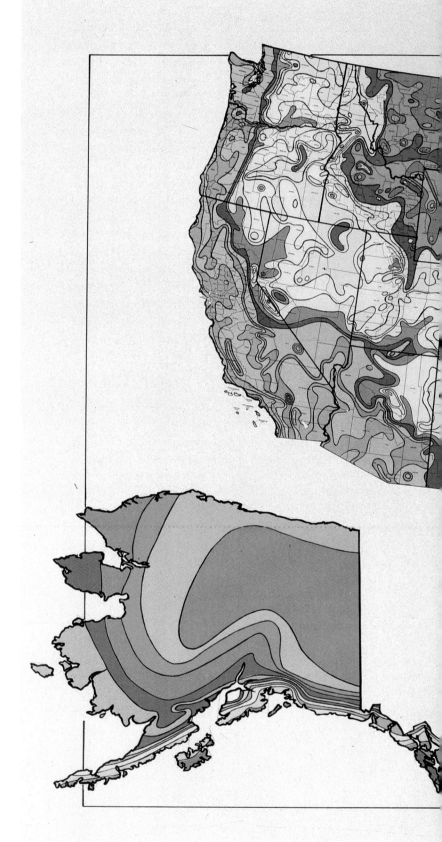

INDEX

(NOTE: Italized page numbers refer to captions.)

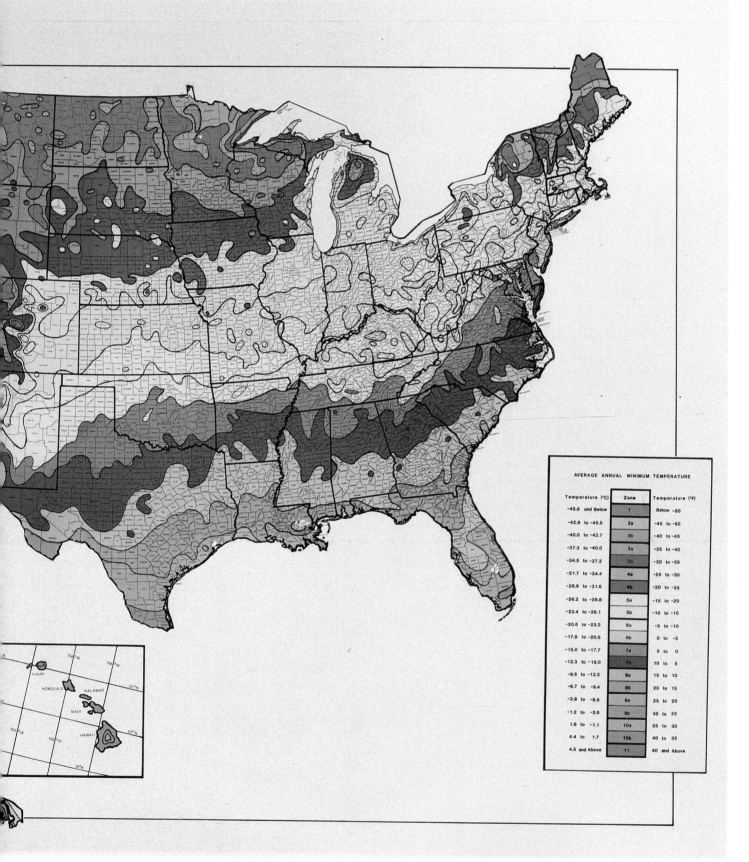

AVERAGE ANNUAL MINIMUM TEMPERATURE

Temperature (°C)	Zone	Temperature (°F)
-45.6 and Below	1	Below -50
-42.8 to -45.5	2a	-45 to -50
-40.0 to -42.7	2b	-40 to -45
-37.3 to -40.0	3a	-35 to -40
-34.5 to -37.2	3b	-30 to -35
-31.7 to -34.4	4a	-25 to -30
-28.9 to -31.6	4b	-20 to -25
-26.2 to -28.8	5a	-15 to -20
-23.4 to -26.1	5b	-10 to -15
-20.6 to -23.3	6a	-5 to -10
-17.8 to -20.5	6b	0 to -5
-15.0 to -17.7	7a	5 to 0
-12.3 to -15.0	7b	10 to 5
-9.5 to -12.2	8a	15 to 10
-6.7 to -9.4	8b	20 to 15
-3.9 to -6.6	9a	25 to 20
-1.2 to -3.8	9b	30 to 25
1.6 to -1.1	10a	35 to 30
4.4 to 1.7	10b	40 to 35
4.5 and Above	11	40 and Above